GENOCIDE & PERSECUTION

| Rwanda

Titles in the Genocide and Persecution Series

GENOCIDE & PERSECUTION

I Rwanda

Noah Berlatsky
Book Editor

Frank Chalk
Consulting Editor

GREENHAVEN PRESS
A part of Gale, Cengage Learning

GALE
CENGAGE Learning·

Farmington Hills, Mich • San Francisco • New York • Waterville, Maine
Meriden, Conn • Mason, Ohio • Chicago

Patricia Coryell, *Vice President & Publisher, New Products & GVRL*
Douglas Dentino, *Manager, New Products*
Judy Galens, *Acquisitions Editor*

© 2015 Greenhaven Press, a part of Gale, Cengage Learning

WCN: 01-100-101

LIBRARY OF CONGRESS CATALOGING-IN-PUBLICATION DATA

Rwanda (2015)
    Rwanda / Noah Berlatsky, book editor.
        pages cm. -- (Genocide and persecution)
    Includes bibliographical references and index.
    ISBN 978-0-7377-7232-6 (hardcover)
1. Rwanda--History--Civil War, 1994--Atrocities. 2. Rwanda--History--Civil War, 1994--Personal narratives. 3. Genocide--Rwanda. 4. Crimes against humanity--Rwanda. 5. Ethnic conflict--Rwanda--History--20th century. I. Berlatsky, Noah, editor of compilation. II. Title. III. Series: Genocide and persecution.
    DT450.435.R823 2015
    967.57104'31--dc23
                                 2014043477

Printed in the United States of America
1 2 3 4 5 6 7 19 18 17 16 15

Contents

Chapter 1: Historical Background on the Rwandan Genocide

Chapter 2: Controversies Surrounding the Rwandan Genocide

Chapter 3: Personal Narratives

Preface

*"For the dead and the living, we must
   bear witness."*

   *Elie Wiesel, Nobel laureate and
   Holocaust survivor*

The histories of many nations are shaped by horrific events involving torture, violent repression, and systematic mass killings. The inhumanity of such events is difficult to comprehend, yet understanding why such events take place, what impact they have on society, and how they may be prevented in the future is vitally important. The Genocide and Persecution series provides readers with anthologies of previously published materials on acts of genocide, crimes against humanity, and other instances of extreme persecution, with an emphasis on events taking place in the twentieth and twenty-first centuries. The series offers essential historical background on these significant events in modern world history, presents the issues and controversies surrounding the events, and provides first-person narratives from people whose lives were altered by the events. By providing primary sources, as well as analysis of crucial issues, these volumes help develop critical-thinking skills and support global connections. In addition, the series directly addresses curriculum standards focused on informational text and literary nonfiction and explicitly promotes literacy in history and social studies.

Each Genocide and Persecution volume focuses on genocide, crimes against humanity, or severe persecution. Material from a variety of primary and secondary sources presents a multinational perspective on the event. Articles are carefully edited and introduced to provide context for readers. The series includes volumes on significant and widely studied events like the Holocaust, as well as events that are less often studied, such as the East Pakistan genocide in what is now Bangladesh. Some volumes focus on multiple events endured by a specific people, such as the Kurds, or multiple events enacted over time by a particular oppressor or in a particular location, such as the People's Republic of China.

Each volume is organized into three chapters. The first chapter provides readers with general background information and uses primary sources such as testimony from tribunals or international courts, documents or speeches from world leaders, and legislative text. The second chapter presents multinational perspectives on issues and controversies and addresses current implications or long-lasting effects of the event. Viewpoints explore such topics as root causes; outside interventions, if any; the impact on the targeted group and the region; and the contentious issues that arose in the aftermath. The third chapter presents first-person narratives from affected people, including survivors, family members of victims, perpetrators, officials, aid workers, and other witnesses.

In addition, numerous features are included in each volume of Genocide and Persecution:

- An annotated **table of contents** provides a brief summary of each essay in the volume.
- A **foreword** gives important background information on the recognition, definition, and study of genocide in recent history and examines current efforts focused on the prevention of future atrocities.
- A **chronology** offers important dates leading up to, during, and following the event.
- **Primary sources**—including historical newspaper accounts, testimony, and personal narratives—are among the varied selections in the anthology.
- **Illustrations**—including a world map, photographs, charts, graphs, statistics, and tables—are closely tied

to the text and chosen to help readers understand key points or concepts.

- **Sidebars**—including biographies of key figures and overviews of earlier or related historical events—offer additional content.
- **Pedagogical features**—including analytical exercises, writing prompts, and group activities—introduce each chapter and help reinforce the material. These features promote proficiency in writing, speaking, and listening skills and literacy in history and social studies.
- A **glossary** defines key terms, as needed.
- An annotated list of international **organizations to contact** presents sources of additional information on the volume topic.
- A **list of primary source documents** provides an annotated list of reports, treaties, resolutions, and judicial decisions related to the volume topic.
- A **for further research** section offers a bibliography of books, periodical articles, and Internet sources and an annotated section of other items such as films and websites.
- A comprehensive subject **index** provides access to key people, places, events, and subjects cited in the text.

The Genocide and Persecution series illuminates atrocities that cannot and should not be forgotten. By delving deeply into these events from a variety of perspectives, students and other readers are provided with the information they need to think critically about the past and its implications for the future.

Foreword

The term *genocide* often appears in news stories and other literature. It is not widely known, however, that the core meaning of the term comes from a legal definition, and the concept became part of international criminal law only in 1951 when the United Nations Convention on the Prevention and Punishment of the Crime of Genocide came into force. The word *genocide* appeared in print for the first time in 1944 when Raphael Lemkin, a Polish Jewish refugee from Adolf Hitler's World War II invasion of Eastern Europe, invented the term and explored its meaning in his pioneering book *Axis Rule in Occupied Europe*.

Humanity's Recognition of Genocide and Persecution

Lemkin understood that throughout the history of the human race there have always been leaders who thought they could solve their problems not only through victory in war, but also by destroying entire national, ethnic, racial, or religious groups. Such annihilations of entire groups, in Lemkin's view, deprive the world of the very cultural diversity and richness in languages, traditions, values, and practices that distinguish the human race from all other life on earth. Genocide is not only unjust, it threatens the very existence and progress of human civilization, in Lemkin's eyes.

Looking to the past, Lemkin understood that the prevailing coarseness and brutality of earlier human societies and the lower value placed on human life obscured the existence of genocide. Sacrifice and exploitation, as well as torture and public execution, had been common at different times in history. Looking toward a more humane future, Lemkin asserted the need to punish— and when possible prevent—a crime for which there had been no name until he invented it.

Legal Definitions of Genocide

On December 9, 1948, the United Nations adopted its Convention on the Prevention and Punishment of the Crime of Genocide (UNGC). Under Article II, genocide

> means any of the following acts committed with intent to destroy, in whole or in part, a national, ethnical, racial or religious group, as such:
>
> (a) Killing members of the group;
>
> (b) Causing serious bodily or mental harm to members of the group;
>
> (c) Deliberately inflicting on the group conditions of life calculated to bring about its physical destruction in whole or in part;
>
> (d) Imposing measures intended to prevent births within the group;
>
> (e) Forcibly transferring children of the group to another group.

Article III of the convention defines the elements of the crime of genocide, making punishable:

> (a) Genocide;
>
> (b) Conspiracy to commit genocide;
>
> (c) Direct and public incitement to commit genocide;
>
> (d) Attempt to commit genocide;
>
> (e) Complicity in genocide.

After intense debate, the architects of the convention excluded acts committed with intent to destroy social, political, and economic groups from the definition of genocide. Thus, attempts to destroy whole social classes—the physically and mentally challenged, and homosexuals, for example—are not acts of genocide under the terms of the UNGC. These groups achieved a belated but very significant measure of protection under international criminal law in the Rome Statute of the International Criminal

Court, adopted at a conference on July 17, 1998, and entered into force on July 1, 2002.

The Rome Statute defined a crime against humanity in the following way:

> any of the following acts when committed as part of a widespread and systematic attack directed against any civilian population:
>
> (a) Murder;
>
> (b) Extermination;
>
> (c) Enslavement;
>
> (d) Deportation or forcible transfer of population;
>
> (e) Imprisonment or other severe deprivation of physical liberty in violation of fundamental rules of international law;
>
> (f) Torture;
>
> (g) Rape, sexual slavery, enforced prostitution, forced pregnancy, enforced sterilization, or any other form of sexual violence of comparable gravity;
>
> (h) Persecution against any identifiable group or collectivity on political, racial, national, ethnic, cultural, religious, gender . . . or other grounds that are universally recognized as impermissible under international law, in connection with any act referred to in this paragraph or any crime within the jurisdiction of this Court;
>
> (i) Enforced disappearance of persons;
>
> (j) The crime of apartheid;
>
> (k) Other inhumane acts of a similar character intentionally causing great suffering, or serious injury to body or to mental or physical health.

Although genocide is often ranked as "the crime of crimes," in practice prosecutors find it much easier to convict perpetrators of crimes against humanity rather than genocide under domestic laws. However, while Article I of the UNGC declares that countries adhering to the UNGC recognize genocide as "a crime under international law which they undertake to prevent and to punish," the Rome Statute provides no comparable international mechanism for the prosecution of crimes against humanity. A treaty would help individual countries and international institutions introduce measures to prevent crimes against humanity, as well as open more avenues to the domestic and international prosecution of war criminals.

The Evolving Laws of Genocide

In the aftermath of the serious crimes committed against civilians in the former Yugoslavia since 1991 and the Rwanda genocide of 1994, the United Nations Security Council created special international courts to bring the alleged perpetrators of these events to justice. While the UNGC stands as the standard definition of genocide in law, the new courts contributed significantly to today's nuanced meaning of genocide, crimes against humanity, ethnic cleansing, and serious war crimes in international criminal law.

Also helping to shape contemporary interpretations of such mass atrocity crimes are the special and mixed courts for Sierra Leone, Cambodia, Lebanon, and Iraq, which may be the last of their type in light of the creation of the International Criminal Court (ICC), with its broad jurisdiction over mass atrocity crimes in all countries that adhere to the Rome Statute of the ICC. The Yugoslavia and Rwanda tribunals have already clarified the law of genocide, ruling that rape can be prosecuted as a weapon in committing genocide, evidence of intent can be absent when convicting low-level perpetrators of genocide, and public incitement to commit genocide is a crime even if genocide does not immediately follow the incitement.

Several current controversies about genocide are worth noting and will require more research in the future:

1. Dictators accused of committing genocide or persecution may hold onto power more tightly for fear of becoming

vulnerable to prosecution after they step down. Therefore, do threats of international indictments of these alleged perpetrators actually delay transfers of power to more representative rulers, thereby causing needless suffering?

2. Would the large sum of money spent for international retributive justice be better spent on projects directly benefiting the survivors of genocide and persecution?

3. Can international courts render justice impartially or do they deliver only "victors' justice," that is the application of one set of rules to judge the vanquished and a different and laxer set of rules to judge the victors?

It is important to recognize that the law of genocide is constantly evolving, and scholars searching for the roots and early warning signs of genocide may prefer to use their own definitions of genocide in their work. While the UNGC stands as the standard definition of genocide in law, the debate over its interpretation and application will never end. The ultimate measure of the value of any definition of genocide is its utility for identifying the roots of genocide and preventing future genocides.

Motives for Genocide and Early Warning Signs

When identifying past cases of genocide, many scholars work with some version of the typology of motives published in 1990 by historian Frank Chalk and sociologist Kurt Jonassohn in their book *The History and Sociology of Genocide*. The authors identify the following four motives and acknowledge that they may overlap, or several lesser motives might also drive a perpetrator:

1. To eliminate a real or potential threat, as in Imperial Rome's decision to annihilate Carthage in 146 B.C.

2. To spread terror among real or potential enemies, as in Genghis Khan's destruction of city-states and people who rebelled against the Mongols in the thirteenth century.

3. To acquire economic wealth, as in the case of the Massachusetts Puritans' annihilation of the native Pequot people in 1637.

4. To implement a belief, theory, or an ideology, as in the case of Germany's decision under Hitler and the Nazis to destroy completely the Jewish people of Europe from 1941 to 1945.

Although these motives represent differing goals, they share common early warning signs of genocide. A good example of genocide in recent times that could have been prevented through close attention to early warning signs was the genocide of 1994 inflicted on the people labeled as "Tutsi" in Rwanda. Between 1959 and 1963, the predominantly Hutu political parties in power stigmatized all Tutsi as members of a hostile racial group, violently forcing their leaders and many civilians into exile in neighboring countries through a series of assassinations and massacres. Despite systematic exclusion of Tutsi from service in the military, government security agencies, and public service, as well as systematic discrimination against them in higher education, hundreds of thousands of Tutsi did remain behind in Rwanda. Government-issued cards identified each Rwandan as Hutu or Tutsi.

A generation later, some Tutsi raised in refugee camps in Uganda and elsewhere joined together, first organizing politically and then militarily, to reclaim a place in their homeland. When the predominantly Tutsi Rwanda Patriotic Front invaded Rwanda from Uganda in October 1990, extremist Hutu political parties demonized all of Rwanda's Tutsi as traitors, ratcheting up hate propaganda through radio broadcasts on government-run Radio Rwanda and privately owned radio station RTLM. Within the print media, *Kangura* and other publications used vicious cartoons to further demonize Tutsi and to stigmatize any Hutu who dared advocate bringing Tutsi into the government. Massacres of dozens and later hundreds of Tutsi sprang up even as Rwandans prepared to elect a coalition government led by moderate political parties, and as the United Nations dispatched a small international military force led by Canadian general Roméo Dallaire to oversee the elections and political transition. Late in 1992, an international human rights organization's investigating team detected the hate propaganda campaign, verified systematic massacres of Tutsi, and warned the international community that Rwanda had already entered the early stages of genocide, to no avail. On April 6, 1994, Rwanda's genocidal killing accelerated at an alarming pace when someone shot down the airplane flying Rwandan president Juvenal Habyarimana home from peace talks in Arusha, Tanzania.

Hundreds of thousands of Tutsi civilians—including children, women, and the elderly—died horrible deaths because the world ignored the early warning signs of the genocide and refused to act. Prominent among those early warning signs were: 1) systematic, government-decreed discrimination against the Tutsi as members of a supposed racial group; 2) government-issued identity cards labeling every Tutsi as a member of a racial group; 3) hate propaganda casting all Tutsi as subversives and traitors; 4) organized assassinations and massacres targeting Tutsi; and 5) indoctrination of militias and special military units to believe that all Tutsi posed a genocidal threat to the existence of Hutu and would enslave Hutu if they ever again became the rulers of Rwanda.

Genocide Prevention and the Responsibility to Protect

The shock waves emanating from the Rwanda genocide forced world leaders at least to acknowledge in principle that the national sovereignty of offending nations cannot trump the responsibility of those governments to prevent the infliction of mass atrocities on their own people. When governments violate that obligation, the member states of the United Nations have a responsibility to get involved. Such involvement can take the form of, first, offering to help the local government change its ways through technical advice and development aid, and second—if the local government persists in assaulting its own people—initiating armed intervention to protect the civilians at risk. In 2005 the United Nations began to implement the Responsibility to Protect initiative, a framework of principles to guide the international community in preventing mass atrocities.

As in many real-world domains, theory and practice often diverge. Genocide and crimes against humanity are rooted in problems that produce failing states: poverty, poor education, extreme nationalism, lawlessness, dictatorship, and corruption. Implementing the principles of the Responsibility to Protect doctrine burdens intervening state leaders with the necessity of addressing each of those problems over a long period of time. And when those problems prove too intractable and complex to solve easily, the citizens of the intervening nations may lose patience, voting out the leader who initiated the intervention. Arguments based solely on humanitarian principles fail to overcome such concerns. What is needed to persuade political leaders to stop preventable mass atrocities are compelling arguments based on their own national interests.

Preventable mass atrocities threaten the national interests of all states in five specific ways:

1. Mass atrocities create conditions that engender widespread and concrete threats from terrorism, piracy, and other forms of lawlessness on the land and sea;
2. Mass atrocities facilitate the spread of warlordism, whose tentacles block affordable access to vital raw materials produced in the affected country and threaten the prosperity of all nations that depend on the consumption of these resources;
3. Mass atrocities trigger cascades of refugees and internally displaced populations that, combined with climate change and growing international air travel, will accelerate the worldwide incidence of lethal infectious diseases;

4. Mass atrocities spawn single-interest parties and political agendas that drown out more diverse political discourse in the countries where the atrocities take place and in the countries that host large numbers of refugees. Xenophobia and nationalist backlashes are the predictable consequences of government indifference to mass atrocities elsewhere that could have been prevented through early actions;

5. Mass atrocities foster the spread of national and transnational criminal networks trafficking in drugs, women, arms, contraband, and laundered money.

Alerting elected political representatives to the consequences of mass atrocities should be part of every student movement's agenda in the twenty-first century. Adam Smith, the great political economist and author of *The Wealth of Nations*, put it best when he wrote: "It is not from the benevolence of the butcher, the brewer, or the baker that we expect our dinner, but from their regard to their own interest." Self-interest is a powerful engine for good in the marketplace and can be an equally powerful motive and source of inspiration for state action to prevent genocide and mass persecution. In today's new global village, the lives we save may be our own.

Frank Chalk

Frank Chalk, who has a doctorate from the University of Wisconsin–Madison, is a professor of history and director of the Montreal Institute for Genocide and Human Rights Studies at Concordia University in Montreal, Canada. He is coauthor, with Kurt Jonassohn, of The History and Sociology of Genocide *(1990); coauthor, with General Roméo Dallaire, Kyle Matthews, Carla Barqueiro, and Simon Doyle, of* Mobilizing the Will to Intervene: Leadership to Prevent Mass Atrocities *(2010); and associate editor of the three-volume Macmillan Reference USA* Encyclopedia of Genocide and Crimes Against Humanity *(2004). Chalk served as president of the International Association of Genocide Scholars from June 1999 to June 2001. His current research focuses on the use of radio and television broadcasting in the incitement and prevention of genocide, and domestic laws on genocide. For more information on genocide and examples of the experiences of people displaced by genocide and other human rights violations, interested readers can consult the websites of the Montreal Institute for Genocide and Human Rights Studies (http://migs.concordia.ca) and the Montreal Life Stories project (www.lifestoriesmontreal.ca).*

World Map

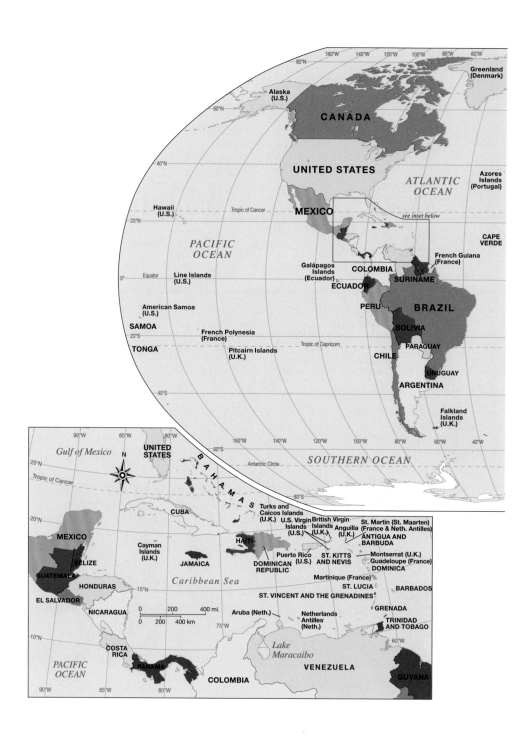

80°N

160°W 140°W 120°W 100°W 80°W 60°W

Greenland
(Denmark)

Alaska
(U.S.)

60°N

CANADA

40°N

UNITED STATES

ATLANTIC
OCEAN

Azores
Islands
(Portugal)

Hawaii
(U.S.)

Tropic of Cancer

20°N

MEXICO

see inset below

CAPE
VERDE

PACIFIC
OCEAN

French Guiana
(France)

Galápagos
Islands
(Ecuador)

COLOMBIA

SURINAME

Equator

0°

Line Islands
(U.S.)

ECUADOR

American Samoa
(U.S.)

PERU

BRAZIL

SAMOA

20°S

BOLIVIA

French Polynesia
(France)

TONGA

Pitcairn Islands
(U.K.)

Tropic of Capricorn

PARAGUAY

CHILE

URUGUAY

ARGENTINA

40°S

Falkland
Islands
(U.K.)

90°W 85°W 80°W

160°W 140°W 120°W 100°W 80°W 60°W 40°W

Gulf of Mexico

N

UNITED
STATES

60°S

Antarctic Circle

SOUTHERN OCEAN

25°N

BAHAMAS

Tropic of Cancer

80°S

CUBA

Turks and
Caicos Islands
(U.K.)

U.S. Virgin
Islands
(U.S.)

British Virgin
Islands
(U.K.)

Anguilla
(U.K.)

St. Martin (St. Maarten)
(France & Neth. Antilles)

20°N

MEXICO

Cayman
Islands
(U.K.)

HAITI

JAMAICA

Puerto Rico
(U.S.)

DOMINICAN
REPUBLIC

ST. KITTS
AND NEVIS

ANTIGUA AND
BARBUDA

Montserrat (U.K.)
Guadeloupe (France)
DOMINICA

BELIZE

GUATEMALA

Caribbean Sea

Martinique (France)

BARBADOS

HONDURAS

15°N

ST. VINCENT AND THE GRENADINES

EL SALVADOR

ST. LUCIA

NICARAGUA

0 200 400 mi.

0 200 400 km

Aruba (Neth.)

Netherlands
Antilles
(Neth.)

GRENADA

TRINIDAD
AND TOBAGO

75°W

COSTA
RICA

60°W

PACIFIC
OCEAN

PANAMA

Lake
Maracaibo

VENEZUELA

GUYANA

10°N

90°W 85°W 80°W

COLOMBIA

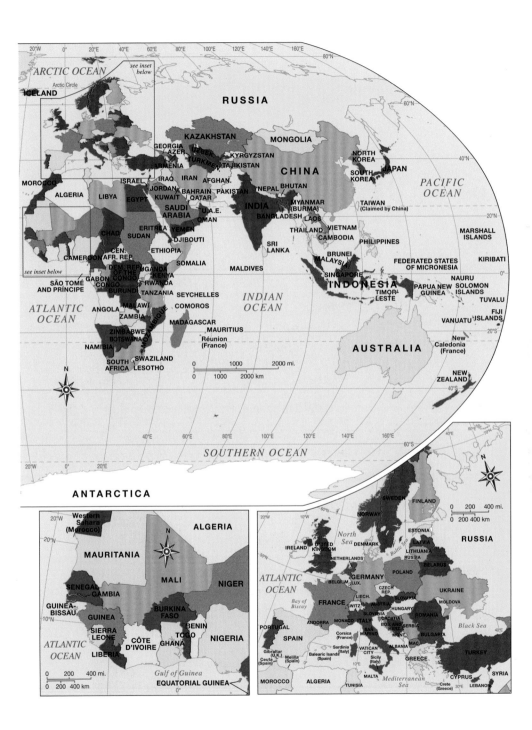

ARCTIC OCEAN

ICELAND

Arctic Circle

see inset below

RUSSIA

KAZAKHSTAN

MONGOLIA

GEORGIA
AZER.
ARMENIA
TURKMEN. NIGER
TAJIKISTAN
KYRGYZSTAN

NORTH KOREA
SOUTH KOREA
JAPAN

CHINA

PACIFIC OCEAN

MOROCCO
ALGERIA
LIBYA
EGYPT
ISRAEL
JORDAN
KUWAIT
IRAQ
IRAN
AFGHAN.
BAHRAIN PAKISTAN
QATAR
SAUDI ARABIA
U.A.E.
OMAN
NEPAL BHUTAN
INDIA
BANGLADESH
MYANMAR (BURMA)
LAOS
TAIWAN (Claimed by China)

MARSHALL ISLANDS

CHAD
ERITREA
SUDAN
YEMEN
DJIBOUTI
ETHIOPIA
SRI LANKA
THAILAND
VIETNAM
CAMBODIA
PHILIPPINES

CEN. AFR. REP.
CAMEROON
SOMALIA
MALDIVES
BRUNEI
MALAYSIA
SINGAPORE

FEDERATED STATES OF MICRONESIA

KIRIBATI

see inset below

GABON
SÃO TOMÉ AND PRÍNCIPE
CONGO
DEM. REP. OF THE CONGO
UGANDA
RWANDA
BURUNDI
KENYA
TANZANIA
SEYCHELLES

INDONESIA
TIMOR-LESTE

PAPUA NEW GUINEA

NAURU
SOLOMON ISLANDS

TUVALU

ATLANTIC OCEAN

ANGOLA
MALAWI
ZAMBIA
MOZAMBIQUE
COMOROS
MADAGASCAR

INDIAN OCEAN

VANUATU

FIJI ISLANDS

ZIMBABWE
BOTSWANA
NAMIBIA
SWAZILAND
SOUTH AFRICA LESOTHO

MAURITIUS
Réunion (France)

AUSTRALIA

New Caledonia (France)

NEW ZEALAND

0   1000   2000 mi.
0 1000 2000 km

N

ANTARCTICA

SOUTHERN OCEAN

Western Sahara (Morocco)
ALGERIA

MAURITANIA

N

MALI

NIGER

SENEGAL
GAMBIA
GUINEA-BISSAU
GUINEA
SIERRA LEONE
CÔTE D'IVOIRE
LIBERIA
BURKINA FASO
TOGO
BENIN
GHANA
NIGERIA

ATLANTIC OCEAN

Gulf of Guinea

EQUATORIAL GUINEA

0   200   400 mi.
0 200 400 km

SWEDEN
FINLAND
NORWAY

0   200   400 mi.
0 200 400 km

N

ESTONIA
North Sea
IRELAND
UNITED KINGDOM
DENMARK
LITHUANIA
LATVIA
RUSSIA
Baltic Sea
BELARUS

RUSSIA

NETHERLANDS
POLAND
GERMANY
BELGIUM LUX.
CZECH REP.
UKRAINE

ATLANTIC OCEAN

Bay of Biscay
FRANCE
SWITZ.
LIECH.
AUSTRIA
HUNGARY
SLOVENIA
CROATIA
MOLDOVA
ROMANIA

ANDORRA
MONACO
ITALY
SAN MARINO
BOS. AND HERZ.
SERBIA
MONT.
BULGARIA

Black Sea

PORTUGAL
SPAIN
Corsica (France)
VATICAN CITY
MAC.
ALBANIA
GREECE
TURKEY

Gibraltar (U.K.)
Ceuta (Spain)
Melilla (Spain)
Balearic Isands (Spain)
Sardinia (Italy)
Sicily (Italy)
MALTA
Mediterranean Sea
CYPRUS
SYRIA
LEBANON
Crete (Greece)

MOROCCO
ALGERIA
TUNISIA

17

Chronology

1890	Germans gain control of Rwanda.
1916	Belgium takes control of Rwanda from Germany. Belgium promotes Tutsis into power at the expense of majority Hutus.
1959	A Hutu rebellion drives the Tutsi elite and tens of thousands of Tutsi citizens from the country.
1962	Rwanda gains formal independence from Belgium, and the majority Hutus gain power.
1963	Tutsi rebels invade from Burundi. Twenty thousand Tutsis are killed in reprisal.
1973	Juvénal Habyarimana stages a coup and becomes president of Rwanda.
1990	The mostly Tutsi rebels of the Rwandan Patriotic Front (RPF), under Tutsi-leader Paul Kagame's command, invade Rwanda from Uganda, sparking a civil war with the Hutu government.
1993	The Arusha Accords are signed between Habyarimana and the RPF. The treaty is supposed to end the civil war and establish a power-sharing government.
April 6, 1994	Habyarimana's plane is shot down, and he and the president of Burundi are killed. The extremist Hutu government

seizes the opportunity to launch a genocide against Tutsis and moderate Hutus. Killings begin the same night.

April 7, 1994   Hutu government forces focus on killing Hutu and Tutsi opponents of the regime in Kigali, killing thousands. They assassinate Prime Minister Agathe Uwilingiyimana, a moderate Hutu, and ten Belgian troops from the UN Assistance Mission in Rwanda (UNAMIR) who are protecting her, prompting Belgium to recall all of its troops.

April 8, 1994   The RPF responds by launching an offensive from northern Rwanda.

April 21, 1994   The UN Security Council reduces UNAMIR forces in Rwanda from 2,548 to 270, despite UNAMIR commander Roméo Dallaire's requests for reinforcements.

May 17, 1994   The UN agrees to strengthen UNAMIR forces to 5,500 troops, though the large-scale massacres of Tutsis are mostly complete.

June 22, 1994   French forces establish a safe zone for refugees in southwestern Rwanda, which is alleged to have also provided a safe escape route for Hutu genocide perpetrators.

July 17, 1994   RPF forces declare victory, having captured Kigali and defeated the Rwandan government, officially ending the genocide, which killed eight hundred thousand in about one hundred days.

1995   Hutus in Zaire (including exiles from Rwanda who participated in the genocide) launch attacks on Tutsis in that country. A UN-appointed international tribunal begins to investigate and prosecute those involved in the Rwandan genocide.

1996   Rwanda's Tutsi government invades Zaire to capture Hutu refugees and force them back to Rwanda.

1997   Rwanda helps to depose Zaire's president, Mobutu Sese Seko. Zaire is renamed Democratic Republic of Congo, and Laurent Kabila becomes its president.

1998   Rwanda changes sides and supports rebel forces against Kabila, because Kabila did not expel extremist Hutus in refugee camps.

2000   Paul Kagame, leader of the RPF, becomes the official president of Rwanda.

2002   Rwanda and Democratic Republic of Congo (DRC) sign a peace deal, in which DRC agrees to disarm Hutus implicated in the 1994 genocide, and Rwanda agrees to pull troops out of DRC.

2003   A new Rwandan constitution is adopted, which bans incitement of ethnic hatred.

CHAPTER 1

Historical Background on the Rwandan Genocide

Chapter Exercises

1. Analyzing Statistics

Question 1: What is the majority ethnic group in Rwanda? What percent of the population are ethnic minorities?

Question 2: Is Rwanda sparsely or densely populated compared to other countries? Which statistic(s) help to make your determination?

Question 3: Is Rwanda a relatively poor or rich country? Which statistic(s) did you use to make your determination?

2. Writing Prompt

Imagine you are a journalist based in Kigali as the genocide in Rwanda is breaking out. Write an article in which you report to an international audience on the events leading up to the genocide and the developments in Rwanda in recent weeks. Come up with a clear and compelling title to grab your audience's attention and include any background information needed to explain the events as well as important names, places, and ideas.

3. Group Activity

Form small groups and discuss the known facts about the campaign to eradicate Tutsis in Rwanda. Have your group write a speech to be delivered at the United Nations after the outbreak of violence in April 1994 describing the genocide and its causes. Suggest specific actions that the international community could take to improve the situation in Rwanda. A representative from each small group may be chosen to read the speech aloud to the larger group.

The Legacy of Colonization and the Roots of the Rwandan Genocide

Timothy Longman

In the following viewpoint, a political science professor provides an account of the background and circumstances of the Rwandan genocide. He maintains that Western colonizers exacerbated ethnic tensions in Rwanda in the early twentieth century by giving power to Tutsis over ethnic Hutus. In postcolonial times, the author writes, Hutus came to power in Rwanda but expelled many Tutsi leaders and citizens, some of whom eventually formed a rebel group that would undermine Hutu authority. According to the author, the resulting tensions erupted in 1994 with a deliberate massacre of Tutsis by the Hutu government, and during this time the Tutsi rebel group managed to seize control of the country. Rwanda has enjoyed stability since 1994, the author reports, but the Tutsi government has been repressive, and reconciliation has been piecemeal. Timothy Longman is the director of the African Studies Center and an associate professor of political science at Boston University.

The 1994 genocide in Rwanda represents one of the clearest cases of genocide in modern history. From early April 1994

Timothy Longman, "The Rwanda Genocide," *Encyclopedia of Genocide and Crimes Against Humanity*, Dinah L. Shelton, ed. Detroit: Macmillan Reference USA, 2005. Copyright © 2005. Reproduced by permission.

through mid-July 1994, members of the small Central African state's majority Hutu ethnic group systematically slaughtered members of the Tutsi ethnic minority. An extremist Hutu regime, fearing the loss of its power in the face of a democracy movement and a civil war, made plans for the elimination of all those—moderate Hutu as well as Tutsi—it perceived as threats to its authority. The genocide ended only when a mostly Tutsi rebel army occupied the country and drove the genocidal regime into exile. Over a period of only one hundred days, as many as one million people lost their lives in the genocide and war—making the Rwandan slaughter one of the most intense waves of killing in recorded history. . . .

Early Instances of Ethnic Violence

Rwanda was colonized by Germany, which ceded the region to the Belgians during World War I. . . . Violent conflict along ethnic lines rarely, if ever, occurred in pre-colonial Rwanda. . . . German and Belgian colonial policies exacerbated the already existing divisions among Hutu, Tutsi, and Twa. Catholic missionaries, who arrived in Rwanda in 1900, influenced the development of ethnic identity in Rwanda. They believed that Rwanda had three distinct racial groups. . . .

These interpretations ultimately shaped how Rwandans saw themselves and understood their group identities; moreover, they had become a basis for policies. German and Belgian colonial administrators practiced ethnic group–based indirect rule. They put power in the hands of Tutsi and gave administrative and political positions to Tutsi, and at the same time eliminated the power of Hutu kings and chiefs. The Belgian colonial administration issued identity cards to all Rwandans that named their ethnicity. In addition the Belgian colonial law of Rwanda dictated that one's ethnicity was the ethnicity of one's father—which effectively eliminated the prior fluid nature of ethnic identities. Occupational and educational opportunities were reserved for Tutsi, whereas Hutu were required to provide forced labor for the Tutsi chiefs. As a result of these and other policies, the Hutu population of Rwanda became increasingly impoverished and embittered. In the 1950s a Hutu elite, supported by progressive Catholic missionaries, emerged to challenge the inequality of Rwandan society. In 1959 a Hutu uprising drove Tutsi chiefs from their positions and thousands of Tutsi citizens of Rwanda into exile. The uprising marked the beginning of the transfer of political power to the majority Hutu. Rwanda gained its independence in 1962. The Hutu-dominated post-independence governments referred to the 1959 uprising as a social revolution. (The current Rwandan government refers to the turbulent events of 1959 as Rwanda's first instance of genocide—though in fact few Tutsi were killed at that time.)

In 1962 Grégoire Kayibanda, the leader of the Party of the Movement for the Emancipation of Hutu (Parmehutu), became Rwanda's president. Kayibanda used ethnic appeals to build his support—thereby creating a tense social environment. When rebel groups that had taken form among the exiled Tutsi attacked the country several times in the early 1960s, Rwandan troops responded by massacring thousands of Tutsi. Thousands more were driven into exile. Ethnic violence erupted in Rwanda again in 1973, partially in response to the 1972 genocide of educated Hutu in neighboring Burundi (which had an ethnic composition similar to that of Rwanda), where Tutsi had retained control. The resulting social disruption in Rwanda was a factor that contributed to the July 1973 coup d'etat that installed army chief Juvenal Habyarimana as the president of Rwanda.

Under Habyarimana, ethnic tensions in Rwanda initially diminished, as the regime focused on attracting international assistance for economic development. The establishment of ethnic quotas in education and employment (which shrank opportunities for Tutsi) appeased Hutu, and the creation of a single political party, the National Revolutionary Movement for Development (MRND), sharply constrained potentially inflammatory political activity. Tutsi were still required to carry identity cards and faced discrimination, but active ethnic tensions diminished. The resulting political calm attracted both internal and international support for Habyarimana, and allowed a decade of steady economic growth. By the mid-1980s, however, among Rwandans, frustration with the Habyarimana regime was on the rise. . . .

The October 1990 invasion of Rwanda by the Rwandan Patriotic Front (RPF) changed the political equation in the country, as it both further compromised the security of the regime and provided an opportunity for Habyarimana and his cohorts to regain popular support by playing the ethnic card. The RPF was a rebel group composed primarily of Tutsi refugees seeking the right to return to Rwanda. . . .

Over the next several years, Habyarimana and his supporters used a cunning two-pronged strategy to improve their political position. On the one hand, they appeased critics by entering into negotiations with the RPF and offering political concessions, including the legalization of opposition parties and the creation of a government of (ostensible) national unity. Yet on the other hand they actively undermined these concessions. They denied opposition politicians real political power as they simultaneously blamed them for any problems that the country faced, such as the economic decline and the growing unemployment resulting from the civil war and an International Monetary Fund (IMF)–imposed austerity program and currency devaluation. Habyarimana's supporters encouraged acts of violence between the members of opposing political parties and were complacent toward an increase in overall criminal violence, then blamed the growing insecurity on the shift to multi-party politics. . . .

The Road to Genocide

Within the powerful clique close to Habyarimana known as the *akazu*, the idea of retaking broad political control via the setting off of large-scale massacres of any and all persons they regarded as threats to the Habyarimana regime was apparently first proposed sometime in 1992. The akazu was composed primarily

Juvénal Habyarimana is shown in 1975, two years after the coup d'état in which he took control of Rwanda. Habyarimana remained in power until his assassination in April 1994. © Keystone/Stringer/Getty Images.

of individuals from Habyarimana's home region in the north of Rwanda, and included descendants of Hutu chiefs who had been displaced by Tutsi during the colonial period—such as some of the relatives of Habyarimana's wife Agathe Kazinga, who for this reason had retained great personal animosity toward Tutsi. Members of the akazu had acquired significant personal wealth and power under Habyarimana's rule, and they were feeling increasingly threatened by political reforms and negotiations with the RPF. Some in the akazu—allegedly by mid-1993—had devised a plan to eliminate both Tutsi and moderate Hutu, as a final solution to the threats against themselves.

A series of events in 1993 shifted popular support in favor of the Habyarimana regime, supplying the popular base that would make the genocide possible. Massacres of Tutsi in the prefectures of Gisenyi and Kibuye in January triggered a major RPF offensive in February, which captured a large swath of territory in northern Rwanda and displaced a million people (mostly Hutu) from the Ruhengeri and Byumba prefectures. With so many people having been displaced and rumors of civilian massacres in areas controlled by the RPF beginning to swirl, public opinion in Rwanda shifted sharply against the RPF. Even as the Habyarimana regime feigned participation in peace negotiations with the RPF and other opposition parties, it sought to undermine the negotiations by fostering anti-Tutsi and anti-RPF sentiments and attributing any concessions it made to the participation of opposition politicians. This strategy effectively split each of the opposition parties, thereby preventing the installation of a new unity government of transition and realigning many southern Hutu with Habyarimana. The final peace agreement, known as the Arusha Accords, signed in August 1993, was widely perceived within Rwanda as having ceded too much to the RPF and having solidified the division of political parties into pro–Arusha Accords and anti–Arusha Accords wings. The anti–Arusha Accords party factions joined with Habyarimana's MRND and the extreme anti-Tutsi party named the Coalition for the Defense of the Republic (CDR) in a loose pro-regime coalition that called itself "Hutu Power."

Hutu Power promoted an ideology that revived much of the anti-Tutsi rhetoric of the Kayibanda period. According to this ideology, Hutu had the right to rule Rwanda because they constituted a majority and because Hutu had a long history in Rwanda (whereas Tutsi had supposedly arrived more recently to conquer and dominate the country). Proponents of the Hutu Power ideology sought to promote a collective memory of Tutsi exploitation of Hutu during the colonial period, and warned that the RPF sought to annul the social revolution of the early 1960s and reassert Tutsi dominance and Hutu subservience. They claimed that all Tutsi within the territory of Rwanda were RPF sympathizers who could not be trusted, and that Hutu who opposed Habyarimana and supported the Arusha Accords were either traitors to the Hutu cause or secretly Tutsi. Associates of Habyarimana established a new quasi-independent radio station in late 1993, Radio Télévision Libre Mille-Collines (RTLM), which broadcast Hutu Power's anti-Tutsi, anti-opposition, and anti-Arusha Accords rhetoric. . . .

Both political and ethnic tensions continued to rise in Rwanda in early 1994. Even as provisions of the Arusha Accords were being implemented, Hutu Power forces sought to scuttle the final transfer of power to a new unity government. The United Nations (UN) Assistance Mission in Rwanda (UNAMIR) stationed international troops in the country to oversee the transition; a battalion of six hundred RPF troops was stationed in Kigali. Rather than reduce its forces, the FAR [Armed Forces of Rwanda] continued to expand in size and acquire arms—receiving weaponry from France, Egypt, and South Africa. In February Faustin Twagiramungu, the transitional prime minister named in the Arusha Accords, narrowly escaped an assassination attempt, while Félicien Gatabazi, the executive secretary of the moderate Social Democratic Party, was assassinated. In response, a crowd that had assembled in Gatabazi's home commune lynched the national chairman of the CDR, Martin Bucyana. These political assassinations intensified the sense of crisis in the country and set the stage for the genocide. Intelligence reports coming out of the United States, France, and Belgium in early 1994 all warned that ethnic and political massacres were an imminent possibility in Rwanda. The commander of UNAMIR forces, General Roméo Dallaire, sent a memo to UN headquarters informing them that he had been informed of the existence of the secret plans of Hutu extremists to carry out genocide. None of these warnings were heeded.

The Genocide Begins

On April 6, 1994, the plane carrying President Habyarimana and Cyprien Ntaryamira, the president of Burundi, who were returning from a meeting in Tanzania that had focused on the implementation of the Arusha Accords, was shot down by surface-to-air missiles as it approached the airport in Kigali, and all on board were killed. The downing of the plane remains shrouded in mystery, since the Rwandan military restricted access to the area of the crash and blocked all serious investigation. Although associates of Habyarimana initially blamed the RPF for the assassination, many other observers believed that troops close to the president had carried out the attack—possibly because of an awareness of Habyarimana's reluctance to permit the plans for genocide (of which he was alleged to have been aware) to move forward, or the perception that he had been too moderate in his attitude toward the RPF. In part because of evidence that was eventually presented before the International Criminal Tribunal for Rwanda (ICTR), many political experts now believe that the RPF, frustrated at the president's resistance toward implementing the Arusha Accords, did in fact fire the rockets that brought down Habyarimana's plane.

Whoever was responsible for the crash, the assassination of Habyarimana served as the spark that set the plans for genocide in motion. Within hours of the crash, members of the presidential guard and other elite troops—carrying hit lists composed of the names of persons perceived to be RPF sympathizers, including prominent Tutsi and Hutu opposition politicians and civil society activists—were spreading throughout the capital. On the morning of April 7, the presidential guard assassinated the Prime Minister, Agathe Uwilingiyimana, a moderate Hutu, along with ten Belgian UNAMIR troops who had been guarding her. On the first day of the genocide, death squads also killed leaders of the predominantly Tutsi Liberal Party and the multiethnic Social Democratic Party, several cabinet ministers, justices of the constitutional court, journalists, human rights activists, and progressive priests.

For the first several days, the murderous attacks took place primarily in Kigali and were focused on prominent individuals, both Hutu and Tutsi, perceived to be opponents of the regime. The international community, at this initial stage of the genocide, construed the violence in Rwanda as an ethnic uprising, a spontaneous popular reaction to the death of the president. Without clearly condemning the political and ethnic violence that was taking place, foreign governments moved to evacuate their nationals from Rwanda. Despite calls from UNAMIR Commander Dallaire to have troop strength increased, the member states of the UN Security Council voted to cut the UNAMIR presence from around 2,500 to a token force of 270, largely because countries such as the United States feared becoming entangled in an intractable conflict that would be reminiscent of the then recent disastrous intervention by the United States in Somalia. Belgium quickly withdrew its forces, and was followed by most other participating countries. From the beginning of the violence, the international community thus promulgated a clear message that it was disinterested and would not act to stop the massacres in Rwanda.

Far from being a spontaneous popular uprising, the 1994 genocide had been carefully planned and coordinated by a small group of government and military officials who used the administrative structure and coercive force of the state to invigorate the genocide and extend it across the country. Following Habyarimana's death, a new interim government composed entirely of Hutu Power supporters had seized control. Once it became clear that the international community was not going to intervene, the death squads moved the genocide into a second phase, expanding the violence until it engulfed the entire country and focusing it more specifically on Tutsi. Using the language of self-defense, the interim government called upon the population to help protect Rwanda from the invading RPF and to root out collaborators and infiltrators within the country. It sent word to regional and local leaders of the *Interahamwe* [Hutu-led paramilitary force] and other militias to move forward with existing "civil self-defense" plans that entailed the elimination of all "threats to security" (understood to mean all Tutsi and, to a lesser extent, moderate Hutu). Political officials had to support the "security" efforts or relinquish their government positions.

Following Habyarimana's death and the start of the civilian massacres, the RPF ended the ceasefire that had been in effect since the previous year and renewed its assault on the country. The RPF troops stationed in Kigali as part of the terms of the Arusha Accords quickly occupied a section of the capital, which became a safe zone for Tutsi and others threatened by the genocidal regime. Other RPF troops advanced on the capital from the north, overtaking the prefecture of Byumba and moving east and south through the prefecture of Kibungo and into the Bugesera region. As RPF leaders were claiming that their offensive was necessary to protect the Tutsi from extermination, their advance across Rwanda provided ideological support for those promoting the genocide. As Rwandans fled in advance of the RPF onslaught, Radio Rwanda and RTLM widely disseminated reports of civilian massacres by the RPF, fueling popular fears of the rebel army.

The genocide in each community followed a pattern. First, the civilian militias raided Tutsi homes and businesses. Fleeing Tutsi were forced to seek refuge in central locations, such as schools, public offices, and churches, where they had been protected during previous waves of violence. Coordinators of the genocide actively exploited the concept of sanctuary and encouraged Tutsi to gather at these places, offering promises

The Twa Ethnic Group

The Twa, once called Pygmies, a term now considered to be derogatory, are believed to be descendants of the original residents of what is now Rwanda. Today they number only about 25,000, less than 1 percent of the total population. The Twa, or Batwa as they call themselves, lived for centuries as hunters and gatherers. When the Hutu moved in and established farms, the Twa moved onto mountain slopes and into forests.

During the period of the Rwandan kingdoms, the Twa were favored in the royal court. Many emerged from the forests to become potters. Some also became dancers at the royal court. They became famous for a dance they performed with Tutsi dancers.

Because of their small stature, the Twa have suffered a great deal of prejudice. They have usually been regarded as inferior and have lived in extreme poverty. Even today, many have to beg to survive. Only 28 percent of Twa children go to primary school, compared with 95 percent for the general population, and far fewer even start secondary school. They also suffered severely during the genocide: an estimated 30 percent were killed, compared with 14 percent of the population overall.

Source: David C. King, Rwanda. *Tarrytown, NY: Marshall Cavendish Benchmark, 2006, p. 75.*

of protection when in fact they were calling Tutsi together for their more efficient elimination. In some communities, a limited number of moderate Hutu were killed early in the violence—as a way of sending a message to other Hutu that they needed to cooperate. Once Tutsi had been gathered, soldiers or police joined with the militia in attacking them: first firing on the crowd and throwing grenades, then systematically finishing off survivors with machetes, axes, and knives. In some cases, buildings teeming with victims were set on fire or demolished. In instances in which communities initially resisted the genocide, militias from neighboring areas arrived on the scene and participated in the attacks until local Hutu joined in the killing. Generally armed only with stones, Tutsi were able to pose effective resistance in only a few locations.

By early May the large-scale massacres were complete, and the genocide in each community moved into a second stage of seeking out survivors. The organizers of the genocide clearly sought in this stage to lessen their own responsibility by implicating a larger segment of society in the killing. Although the massacres were carried out by relatively limited groups of militia members and members of the armed forces, all adult men were expected to participate in roadblocks and nightly patrols. People passing through roadblocks were required to show their identity cards. If a person's card stated that his or her ethnicity was Tutsi, he or she was killed on the spot. If a person had no card, he or she was assumed to be Tutsi. Persons who looked stereotypically Tutsi were almost certainly killed. The military patrols ostensibly searched for perpetrators, but they actually looked for surviving Tutsi who were hiding in communities. Many Hutu risked their own lives to protect Tutsi friends and family. The patrols searched homes where Tutsi were believed to be hiding, and if Tutsi were found, the patrols sometimes killed both Tutsi and the Hutu who were harboring them. Twa, who were a minuscule minority of the Rwandan population, were rarely targets of the genocide and in many communities participated in the killing in an effort to improve their social status.

The RPF Gains Control of Rwanda

From the vantage point of the Hutu Power elite, the genocide, although effective at eliminating internal dissent, proved to be a terrible military strategy, as it drained resources and diverted attention from the RPF assault. Better armed and better organized, the RPF swiftly subdued FAR troops. It advanced across eastern Rwanda, then marched west, capturing the former royal capital Nyanza, on May 29; the provisional capital Gitarama, on June 13;

and Kigali, on July 4. As it advanced, the RPF liberated Tutsi still being harbored in large numbers in places such as Nyanza and Kabgayi, but they also carried out civilian massacres in many communities they occupied, sometimes after gathering victims for supposed public meetings. Much of the population fled the RPF advance. As the RPF occupied eastern Rwanda, nearly one million refugees fled into Tanzania, while in July, over one million fled into Zaire.

After initially refusing to intervene in Rwanda and to stop the genocide, the UN Security Council, on May 17, authorized the creation of an expanded international force, UNAMIR II— but by the time the force was ready to deploy, the genocide was over. The RPF, angry at international neglect and believing that it could win an outright victory, rejected the idea of a new international intervention. In mid-June France, which had been a close ally of the regime that turned genocidal, intervened in Rwanda, supposedly to stop the massacres—but it also wished to prevent an absolute RPF victory. French forces established the "Zone Turquoise" in southeastern Rwanda, which they administered for over a month after the RPF had occupied the rest of Rwanda. Nearly two million people gathered in camps for the internally displaced and came under French protection. The French presence also enabled many of the organizers of the genocide, as well as the armed forces, to flee safely into Zaire with their weapons.

On July 17, 1994, the RPF declared victory and named a new interim government. The post-genocide Rwandan government faced the inordinately daunting task of rebuilding a country that had been devastated by violence. The exact number of people killed in the genocide and war remains disputed, and ranges from 500,000 to over a million, with serious disagreement over the portion killed by the RPF and the portion killed by the genocidal regime. Whatever the exact number of dead, the loss of life was massive and the impact on society immeasurable. The RPF, seeking wider popular support, based the new government loosely on the Arusha Accords and appointed a multiethnic slate of ministers from the former opposition parties that included a Hutu president and prime minister. Real power, however, remained firmly in RPF hands, with Defense Minister and Vice President Paul Kagame widely acknowledged as the ultimate authority in the country.

The RPF, which became Rwanda's new national army, took as its first main task the taking of control over the territory, which it did with considerable brutality. The RPF summarily executed hundreds of people who were suspected of involvement in the genocide, and arrested thousands more. Following the late August departure of French forces, the RPF sought to close the camps for the internally displaced. It used force in some cases, such as in its attack on the Kibeho camp in April 1995, in which several thousand civilians died. The refugee camps just across the border in Zaire continued to pose a security threat for the new government, as members of the former FAR and citizen militias living in the camps used the camps as a base from which to launch raids on Rwanda. In mid-1996 the RPF sponsored an antigovernment rebellion in eastern Zaire by the Alliance of Democratic Forces for the Liberation of Congo-Zaire (ADFL). The RPF itself attacked the refugee camps. The RPF killed thousands of refugees who sought to go deeper into Zaire rather than return to Rwanda. With support from the RPF and troops from Uganda and Burundi, the ADFL swiftly advanced across Zaire, driving President Mobutu Sese-Sekou from power in early 1997.

RPF Interests Undermine Reconciliation

After taking power, the new government of Rwanda set about rebuilding the country's physical infrastructure, but it also committed itself to reconstructing the society. The establishment of the principle of accountability for the genocide and a repudiation of the principle of impunity were primary goals. By the late 1990s the government had imprisoned 120,000 people under the accusation of participation in the genocide. Although considerable effort was put into rebuilding the judicial system, trials of persons accused of genocide proceeded very slowly—beginning only in December 1996 and with fewer than five thousand cases tried by 2000. Responding to the need to expedite trials, but also hoping more effectively to promote accountability and reconciliation, the government decided in 2000 to implement a new judicial process, called *gacaca*, based loosely on a traditional Rwandan dispute resolution mechanism. The new gacaca courts, the first of which began to operate in June 2002, consist of panels of popularly elected lay judges from every community in the country. The panels preside at public meetings, at which all but the most serious genocidal crimes are tried. Beginning in 2003, the government began to release provisionally thousands of people who had had no formal charges brought against them or who had confessed to participation in the genocide (and would therefore be given reduced sentences). In addition to judicial strategies, the government has sought to promote reconciliation by promulgating a revised understanding of Rwandan history that emphasizes a unified national identity; creating reeducation camps for returning refugees, released prisoners, entering university students, and newly elected government officials; establishing memorials and annual commemorations of the genocide; changing the national anthem, flag, and seal; decentralizing the political structure; and adopting a new constitution.

Efforts to promote reconciliation have been undermined by the RPF's continuing mistrust of the population and its desire to retain control. The government has been highly intolerant of dissent, accusing critics of supporting the ideology of division and genocide. The government has harassed, outlawed, and co-opted human rights organizations, religious groups, and other segments of civil society. Journalists have been harassed and arrested. All political parties but the RPF have been tightly controlled. Power has become increasingly concentrated in the hands of the RPF and of Tutsi, and Paul Kagame has amassed and continues to amass increasing personal power. Kagame assumed the presidency in 2000. A putative "democratic transition" in 2003 actually served to consolidate RPF control over Rwanda.

The international community, plagued by guilt over its failure to stop the genocide, has been highly forgiving of the human rights abuses of the RPF, generally treating the abuses as an understandable or even necessary occurrence in the aftermath of genocide. It has given backing and assistance both to the camps in Zaire and the reconstruction of Rwanda. The main outcome of the international reaction to the Rwandan genocide was the creation of the ICTR, based in Arusha, Tanzania. Created by the UN Security Council in late 1994, the ICTR is entrusted with trying the chief organizers of the 1994 genocide as well as RPF officials responsible for war crimes. Despite a slow start, the ICTR has tried or at least holds in its custody many of the most prominent officials of the former Rwandan regime. No RPF officials have yet come into ICTR custody.

Ten years after the 1994 genocide, ethnic relations in Rwanda remain tense. The government has become increasingly intolerant of dissent, and a steady flow of individuals has sought political asylum outside Rwanda. Although initially these exiles were mostly Hutu, they now include many Tutsi, including genocide survivors as well as RPF members who have fallen afoul of Kagame. These exiles could eventually become a basis for a serious challenge to the present regime. The constraints that have been put on open communication within Rwanda have hampered discussions about the genocide and its causes, but political reforms and an emphasis on national unity, as well as the active use of security forces, have helped to maintain peace in the country.

Rwandan Rebels Offer Cease-Fire, but Land, Ethnic Issues Simmer

Robert M. Press

In the following viewpoint, a reporter describes a 1990 flare-up of civil-war violence between the Hutu government of General Juvénal Habyarimana and Tutsi rebels. The violence was fueled by longstanding ethnic resentments between the majority Hutu and the Tutsi, who formerly controlled the country. The author adds that tensions were exacerbated by factors such as overcrowding in Rwanda and the decline in value of coffee, Rwanda's major crop. The situation was complicated by the large numbers of Rwandan refugees in surrounding countries, most of whom were Tutsis who had fled Hutu violence in the 1970s. When this viewpoint was originally published, Robert M. Press was a staff writer for the Christian Science Monitor.

One of Africa's smallest countries, Rwanda has seen some of the continent's biggest massacres of the past 31 years. Now the killing has begun anew, sparked by the same divisive issues of the past: scarcity of land and ethnic hatred.

The latest round of violence began Oct. 1, when well-armed Rwandan refugees living in Uganda invaded Rwanda in an attempt to overthrow the government. Ugandan President Yow-eri Museveni said the rebels, mainly Rwandan refugees from the minority Tutsi tribe, have told him that they would agree to an immediate cease-fire.

Maj. Gen. Juvénal Habyarimana, Rwanda's president, on Monday ruled out peace talks with rebels until a cease-fire was firmly in place. But settlement of the land and ethnic issues is likely to take years.

Rwanda is a tiny, landlocked country about the size of West Virginia, but with some 8 million people, making it one of the most crowded countries in the world. Both the cities and the mountainous rural areas are packed. A desperate search for farmland has forced farmers to cultivate right up the sides of mountains and steep hills. "The land is saturated," says René Le-Marchand, a professor at the University of Florida.

Now thousands of Rwandan rebels, many of them refugees who were serving as mercenaries in Uganda's military, want to gain power and give the estimated 250,000 to 1 million Rwan-dan refugees the right to go home. But "there's simply no room for a massive influx of refugees into the country," says Mr. Le-Marchand, a Rwanda expert. Longstanding ethnic hatred has also divided the country. Most of the rebels are Tutsi. They com-prise only 10 to 15 percent of Rwanda's population, but ruled the country as a kingdom from the 16th century until 1959. That year, the Hutu, comprising about 85 to 90 percent of the popula-tion, overthrew their feudal masters, massacring many Tutsi.

The Hutu formed a government and have ruled since then. In 1973, General Habyarimana, a northern Hutu and then minis-ter of defense, seized power from the first Hutu president. From time to time, there have been further flare-ups between the Hutu majority and the tall Tutsi minority, resulting in more massacres. Tutsi are resented by many Hutu as an educated elite who are often successful in business. According to critics of the Rwandan government, Tutsi are blocked from high-level civil service or Army posts.

As a result of the massacres, hundreds of thousands of Tutsi fled. Many today live in countries around Rwanda, including Zaire, Tanzania, and Uganda. Some became mercenaries, working for Zaire's government and assisting Ugandan President Museveni's successful guerrilla movement in the mid-1980s. Having worked their way up to key positions in the Ugandan military,

the Rwandan mercenaries had access to large amounts of weapons, which they took with them to invade Rwanda.

"People were complaining about them [the Rwandan mercenaries] and their mistreatment of Ugandans," says a Ugandan

A woman works in the terraced fields of the mountainous Western Province of Rwanda. Overcrowding has forced farmers into higher terrain in search of available farmland. © Stuart Forster/Alamy.

official in Kampala, Uganda's capital. Museveni denies complicity in the rebel invasion of Rwanda.

A Rwandan rebel supporter contacted by phone in Uganda told the *Monitor*: "We want to return and stop the injustice. . . . The government has been so exploitive. . . . There's no free elections. . . . Social services are not available to all. . . . People can't get employment or education."

The Tutsi rebels claim to have Hutu fighting with them. It is unclear to what extent this is true, but it does appear that many Hutu are strongly critical of the Hutu government. They claim it favors only Hutu from the president's home area in the north. A Western diplomat who has lived in Rwanda agrees that Habyarimana favors his own clan. A well-educated Hutu interviewed in Nairobi agrees: The government stays in power through an "efficient system of repression. . . . There's a lot of discontent in the country among Hutu."

Jean Paul Harroy, a scholar at the University of Brussels, says Habyarimana's government is "good—and serious about development." Rwanda acts no differently from most governments in favoring the president's clan, he says.

Rwanda's real problem, he adds, is declining world prices for coffee, the main cash crop. As for the population crisis, Mr. Harrow says the United Nations and other donors could help relocate many Rwandans to less-populated regions, such as parts of Zaire.

In their invasion, Tutsi rebels counted on discontent to bring many Rwandan Hutu to their side. This has not happened. Instead, both Hutu and Tutsi civilians have fled to Uganda and Kigali, Rwanda's capital.

In Nairobi, Rwandan Ambassador Cyprien Habimana denied reports that Rwandan troops had massacred civilians. All civilians—"every one" of them—had fled the area by Oct. 2, one day after the rebel invasion, he told reporters. But an international development official told the *Monitor* that his organization was working in that area up to mid-October and had seen

THE RPF TAKEOVER OF RWANDA

Rwanda's genocide began on April 7, 1994. The following day, Tutsi-led forces under the Rwandan Patriotic Front (RPF) began their offensive from the north. Their success in claiming Rwanda in July effectively ended the genocide.

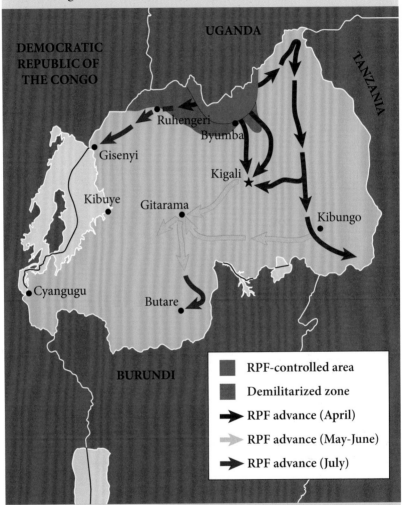

Based on Alan J. Kuperman, *The Limits of Humanitarian Intervention: Genocide in Rwanda*. Washington DC: Brookings Institution Press, 2001, p. 43.

Source: Lemurbaby, "RPF Advance Rwandan Genocide 1994," Wikimedia Commons. http://commons.wikimedia.org.

Rwandan civilians. Away from battle zones, other massacres of Hutu civilians have been reported. Mr. Habimana says his government wants European nations to set up a peace-keeping force once a cease-fire is arranged. And just prior to the outbreak of war, he says, his government began moving toward multiparty elections.

The Arusha Accords Attempt to End Violence in Rwanda

Republic of Rwanda and the Rwandese Patriotic Front

The following viewpoint consists of excerpts from the Arusha Accords—the peace agreement between the Hutu-dominated government of Rwanda and the Rwandese Patriotic Front (also called the Rwandan Patriotic Front), a Tutsi rebel group. The accords sought to end the 1990–1993 civil war that preceded the Rwandan genocide. In the accords, both sides agree to a national unity government that will uphold the peace. They also commit to the rule of law as a guarantor of national unity. National unity is described in the agreement as a rejection of any form of discrimination by ethnicity, regional origin, sex, or religion. The agreement further upholds the right of all Rwandan refugees to return to their country.

Peace Agreement Between the Government of the Republic of Rwanda and the Rwandese Patriotic Front

The Government of the Republic of Rwanda on the one hand, and the Rwandese Patriotic Front on the other;

Firmly resolved to find a political negotiated solution to the war situation confronting the Rwandese people since 1st October, 1990;

Considering and appreciating the efforts deployed by the countries of the Sub-region with a view to helping the Rwandese people to recover peace;

Referring to the numerous high-level meetings held respectively at Mwanza, United Republic of Tanzania, on 17th October, 1990, in Gbadolite, Republic Zaire, on 26th October, 1990, in Goma, Republic of Zaire, on 20th November, 1990, in Zanzibar, United Republic of Tanzania, on 17th February, 1991, in Dar-es-Salaam, United Republic of Tanzania, on 19th February, 1991 and from 5th to 7th March, 1993;

Considering that all these meetings aimed first and foremost at establishing a ceasefire so as to enable the two parties to look for a solution to the war through direct negotiations;

Noting the N'sele [Republic of Zaire] Ceasefire Agreement, of 29th March, 1991 as amended in Gbadolite on 16th September, 1991 and at Arusha [United Republic of Tanzania] on 12th July, 1992;

Reaffirming their unwavering determination to respect principles underlying the Rule of Law which include democracy, national unity, pluralism, the respect of fundamental freedoms and rights of the individual;

Considering that these principles constitute the basis and consistency of a lasting peace awaited by the Rwandese people for the benefit of the present and future generations;

Noting the Protocol of Agreement on the Rule of Law signed at Arusha on 18th August, 1992;

Considering that the two parties accepted the principle of power-sharing within the framework of a Broad-Based Transitional Government;

Noting the Protocols of Agreement on Power-Sharing signed at Arusha respectively on 30th October, 1992, and on 9th January, 1993;

Considering that the conflictual situation between the two parties can only be brought to an end through the formation of one and single National Army and a new National Gendarmerie from forces of the two warring parties;

Noting of the Protocol of Agreement on the integration of Armed Forces of both Parties, signed at Arusha on 3rd August, 1993;

Recognizing that the unity of the Rwandese people cannot be achieved until a definitive solution to the problem of Rwandese refugees is found and that the return of Rwandese refugees to their country is an inalienable right and constitutes a factor for peace and national unity and reconciliation;

Noting the Protocol of Agreement on the repatriation of Rwandese refugees and the Resettlement of Displaced Persons, signed at Arusha on 9th June, 1993;

Resolved to eradicate and put a definite end to all the root causes which gave rise to the war;

Have, at the conclusion of the Peace Talks held in Arusha, United Republic of Tanzania, between 10th July, 1992 and 24th June, 1993 as well as Kinihira, Republic of Rwanda from 19th to 25th July, 1993 under the aegis of the Facilitator, His Excellency Ali Hassan MWINYI, President of the United Republic of Tanzania, in the presence of the Representative of the Mediator, His Excellency, MOBUTU SESE SEKO, President of the Republic of Zaire as well as Representatives of the Current Chairmen of the OAU [Organization of African Unity], His Excellency Abdou DIOUF, President of the Republic of Senegal, and Hosni MUBARAK, President of the Arab Republic of Egypt, the Secretary General of the OAU, Dr. Salim Ahmed SALIM, the Secretary General of the United Nations, Dr. Boutros Boutros GHALI and Observers representing Federal Republic of Germany, Belgium, Burundi, the United States of America, France, Nigeria, Uganda and Zimbabwe;

Calling the International Community to witness;

Hereby agree on the following provisions:

The Reaction in Rwanda to the Arusha Accords

The peace accords signed by the government and the RPF [Rwandan Patriotic Front] in Arusha [Tanzania] in August 1993 were designed to end the war, to create a new coalition government inclusive of the RPF, and to integrate the RPF into the Rwandan armed forces. But the Arusha Accords were widely unpopular with Rwanda. Rifts emerged within the opposition parties between supporters and opponents of the accords, and after the first Hutu president of Burundi, Melchior Ndadaye, was killed in a coup attempt in October 1993, a full-scale political realignment occurred. A large portion of Hutu politicians formerly opposed to Habyarimana joined the president's supporters in a broad coalition known as 'Hutu Power,' leaving politically vulnerable the small remaining group of moderate Hutu and the Tutsi, who nearly universally supported the Arusha Accords.

Timothy Longman, "Obstacles to Peacebuilding in Rwanda," in Taisier M. Ali and Robert O. Matthews, eds., Durable Peace: Challenges for Peacebuilding in Africa. *Toronto: University of Toronto Press, 2004, p. 67.*

Article 1

The war between the Government of the Republic of Rwanda and the Rwandese Patriotic Front is hereby brought to an end. . . .

Article 3

The two parties also agree that the Constitution of 10th June, 1991 and the Arusha Peace Agreement shall constitute indissolubly the Fundamental Law that shall govern the Country during the Transition period. . . .

Article 4

In case of conflict between the provisions of the Fundamental Law and those of other Laws and Regulations, the provisions of the Fundamental Law shall prevail.

Article 5

The Government of the Republic of Rwanda and the Rwandese Patriotic Front undertake to make every possible effort to ensure that the present Peace Agreement is respected and implemented.

They further undertake to spare no effort to promote National Unity and Reconciliation. . . .

Protocol of Agreement Between the Government of the Republic of Rwanda and the Rwandese Patriotic Front on the Rule of Law

Signed at Arusha on 18 August 1992.

Preamble:

The Government of the Republic of Rwanda and the Rwandese Patriotic Front,

Reaffirming that the Rule of Law, the principle of the establishment of which was agreed upon by the signatories of the present Protocol of Agreement, in accordance with Article V of the N'sele Agreement, as amended in Gbadolite, on the 16th of September, 1991 and in Arusha on the 12th of July, 1992, shall characterize the political life in our country;

Considering that the Rule of Law implies that nobody, including the authorities, is above the law and that the laws must respect the fundamental rights of the citizens;

Reaffirming that the Rule of Law does not mean merely a formal legality which assures regularity and consistency in the achievement and enforcement of democratic order, and which is first and foremost and fundamentally characterised by justice based on the recognition and full acceptance of the supreme value of the human personality and guaranteed by institutions providing a framework for its fullest expression;

Convinced that the Rule of Law:

- is the best guarantee of national unity, the respect of the fundamental freedoms and rights of the individual:
- is a concrete manifestation of democracy;
- hinges on national unity, democracy, pluralism and respect for human rights;

Have agreed as follows:

Chapter I: National Unity

Article 1. National unity must be based on equality of all citizens before the law, equal opportunities in all fields including the economic field and respect for fundamental rights as stipulated, notably, in the Universal Declaration of Human Rights and in the African Charter on Human and Peoples' Rights.

Article 2. National unity implies that the Rwandese people, as constituent elements of the Rwandese nation, are one and indivisible. It also implies the necessity to fight all obstacles to national unity, notably, ethnicism, regionalism, integrism and intolerance which subordinate the national interest to ethnic, regional, religious and personal interest.

Article 3. National unity entails the rejection of all exclusions and any form of discrimination based notably, on ethnicity, region, sex and religion. It also entails that all citizens have equal opportunity of access to all the political, economic and other advantages, which access must be guaranteed by the State.

Article 4. The two parties acknowledge that the national unity of the people of Rwanda cannot be achieved without a definitive solution to the problem of Rwandese refugees. They recognize that the return of the Rwandese refugees to their country is an inalienable right and represents a factor of peace, unity and national reconciliation. They undertake not to hinder the free exercise of this right by the refugees.

Violence Erupts in Rwanda's Capital

Lindsey Hilsum

The following viewpoint reports on the chaotic beginning of the Rwandan genocide. The author observes that soldiers and roving gangs began attacking and murdering Tutsis in the capital city of Kigali in response to the assassination of Rwanda's Hutu president. She notes that targets of the attacks include political opponents of the regime, members of religious organizations, and Tutsis. Belgium began efforts to organize a peacekeeping force, according to the author, but the scant international intervention was focused on getting foreign nationals out of Rwanda. Lindsey Hilsum is the international editor for Channel 4 News in Great Britain. She was a journalist in Rwanda at the start of the Rwandan genocide in 1994.

Thousands of bodies were seen lying in the streets of Kigali, the Rwandan capital, yesterday [April 8, 1994] after a two-day orgy of violence and looting following the deaths of the presidents of Rwanda and the neighbouring republic of Burundi.

The Belgian government was leading attempts to assemble an international force to go to its former colony, where the com-

UN troops escort a convoy of foreign civilians evacuating Rwanda on April 11, 1994, a few days after violence broke out in the country. © Scott Peterson/Liaison/Getty Images.

mander of a Belgian UN peacekeeping contingent said last night a ceasefire was being negotiated.

The president of the UN Security Council, Colin Keating, reporting an improvement in the situation, said early today an agreement had been reached on a ceasefire. He added that various factions had agreed on the appointment of an interim government, and had chosen a president, prime minister and five ministers.

But it appeared that the priority of any foreign operation would be to airlift foreigners, not to disarm forces which have been using weapons ranging from machetes to artillery.

The US, whose ambassador's residence is under attack, ordered Americans to leave Rwanda and made plans for an evacuation, the US deputy assistant secretary of state, Prudence Bushnell, told a State Department news briefing. And Canada will send a military transport plane to evacuate about 200 Canadian citizens, foreign ministry officials said.

Religious Officials and Foreigners Are Among the Dead

An International Red Cross official who saw the bodies littering the streets also reported finding about 350 bodies at the central hospital and the Vatican ambassador in Kigali said that at least 25 Rwandan priests and nuns have been murdered.

In one incident, soldiers entered a religious centre, locked six priests and nine novice nuns in a room and then killed them. Two Belgian Jesuits were spared.

Belgium was talking to France, the US and the UN about a joint military operation to take and hold Kigali airport.

Belgian paratroops were standing by and 8,000 French troops in the Central African Republic were on alert. At least 10 Belgian UN soldiers were killed by the rebel forces on Thursday after the aircraft carrying the Rwandan and Burundian leaders back from peace talks was brought down by unknown assailants.

A French serviceman and his wife, among several hundred French nationals in Kigali, have also been killed, Radio France Internationale reported.

As Rwandan soldiers pursued their mission of vengeance for what they regard as Wednesday's [April 6, 1994] assassination of President Juvenal Habyarimana, the dead were also found in people's gardens, according to the chief delegate to the International Committee of the Red Cross, Philippe Gaillard, who was able to tour some of the city.

"Many others have been wounded, but the hospital can't cope," he said. "Only one surgeon is working. There are already 350 bodies in the hospital morgue."

Another eyewitness spoke of people dumping bodies outside the hospital morgue.

Mr Gaillard said the soldiers roaming Kigali's streets and setting up roadblocks were respecting the emblem of the Red Cross and allowing teams to move around the city.

Aid agencies reported that refugees were beginning to flee into neighbouring countries after dozens of reports of atrocities, many attributed to the presidential guard, but some allegedly committed by bands of lawless armed youths.

Tutsis Are Not the Only Target

It is not clear why religious communities are being targeted. Soldiers who belong to the late President Habyarimana's majority Hutu tribe have been going from house to house kidnapping and killing minority Tutsis, but the priests and nuns were said to be of both tribes.

Nor is it clear who is a Hutu and who is a Tutsi. A Rwandan journalist, Nestor Serushago, described how youths armed with knives attacked a young couple with a baby, because, although they were Hutus, they looked like Tutsis.

People who support political parties which opposed the late president are also being targeted. A local aid worker said three members of her family who supported the opposition Liberal Party were taken from their homes and killed.

A spokesman for the UN peacekeeping force in Kigali said the fighting had been between members of the rebel Rwanda Patriotic Front and troops of the presidential guard.

However, other sources said that the three sections of the security forces—the gendarmes, the army and the presidential guard—had also been fighting among themselves.

As dusk fell, military chiefs and the few politicians who had not gone into hiding or been killed were still in a meeting. They were reported to be trying to establish a crisis committee to run the country and restore law and order.

The RPF Takes Control of Rwanda as Millions Flee

Robert Block

In the following viewpoint, originally published in 1994, the author reports on the success of the Rwandan Patriotic Front (RPF), which defeated the Hutu government and took control of Rwanda following the genocide. The leader of the RPF, Major-General Paul Kagame, has declared peace, the author notes, even though Hutu refugees are still fleeing Rwanda. The author maintains that ethnic tensions exacerbated by the genocide continue to be a concern, and that the RPF is at odds with French forces, which have established safe zones into which Hutu refugees, including some who participated in the genocide, have fled. When this viewpoint was originally published, Robert Block was a journalist for The Independent.

The war in Rwanda is supposedly over. The military commander of the rebel Rwandese Patriotic Front (RPF), Major-General Paul Kagame, yesterday announced that his mainly Tutsi forces had routed the extremist Hutu government army and were now the undisputed victors of one of history's bloodiest conflicts.

'We have captured all of Rwanda up to the French protection zone (in the south-west of the country) and the ceasefire is effectively in place,' a confident-looking General Kagame told journalists in the Rwandan capital. Dressed in fatigues, General Kagame said that he hoped that an end to the fighting would stop the exodus of hundreds of thousands of Rwandans which is overwhelming relief agencies and threatening a humanitarian catastrophe of unprecedented scale.

Yet despite the apparent good news, serious doubts remain over whether the war is really over or just entering a new phase. UN officials and relief workers say that a ceasefire in itself is no longer enough to reconcile a country so badly divided. A ceasefire may silence the guns but it will do little to heal the country and stem the bloodshed unless the RPF can win Hutu hearts and minds.

The announcement of the truce did little to stem the tidal wave of humanity fleeing Rwanda. The flow of displaced people

Shortly after being named the new Hutu president of Rwanda, Pasteur Bizimungu (left) chats with Paul Kagame, the commander of the Rwandan Patriotic Front, on July 19, 1994. © Alexander Joe/AFP/Getty Images.

Paul Kagame

Paul Kagame emerged as an internationally renowned figure during his leadership of the military resistance that cut short the Rwandan genocide in July 1994. The genocide had marked the horrifying culmination of decades of ethnically framed massacres in post-independence Rwanda between the majority ethnic group of Hutu, who totalled roughly 85 percent of the population, and the minority ethnic Tutsi, who constituted around 15 percent. Upon successfully leading the Rwandese Patriotic Front (RPF) to victory, Kagame became vice-president of Rwanda, a formidable responsibility after over 800,000 Tutsi and politically moderate Hutu had been systematically massacred during a three-month span in one of the world's poorest countries. In 2000 he was appointed president but had since been the subject of intensifying criticism regarding his government's record in terms of human rights abuses and profiteering among the elite. Nonetheless, to some degree Kagame

has now been joined by Rwandans who have taken refuge in the French 'safety zone'. Already 100,000 people have crossed from south-west Rwanda to the Zairean border town of Bukavu, according to the International Committee of the Red Cross. UN sources say that another 1.3 million people are on the roads, heading for Cyangugu, the Rwandan town just across the border from Bukavu.

An estimated 1 million Hutus have already crossed into Goma, Zaire, further north. The influx of another 1 million people to Bukavu will completely sabotage the already inadequate international humanitarian response. 'This has the potential of being far worse than what is happening up there (in Goma),' said Charles Petrie of the UN Rwanda Emergency Office. The RPF now says that there is no need for a protection zone since the militias and the Hutu army have now been routed. They are demanding access to the area where former Hutu government represented an important element of the "African Renaissance" of forward looking politicians and had institutionalized a set of economic reforms that received the stamp of approval of the international financial institutions.

Born in Gitarama Prefecture, Rwanda, in October 1957, Kagame was the youngest of a Tutsi family of four sisters and one other brother. His father was from a privileged Tutsi background drawing on familial relations with King Rudahigwa of Rwanda, and his mother was intimately related to the King's wife. Despite these elite connections the Kagame family was forced to flee Rwanda two years after Paul's birth in the face of ethnically framed violence by Hutu extremists. This very early experience of life on the move would go on to typify much of Kagame's life until mid-1994.

Liam Campling, "Kagame, Paul," Contemporary Black Biography, vol. 54. Detroit: Gale, 2006, pp 76–79.

officials deemed responsible for orchestrating the slaughter of 500,000 people, mainly Tutsis, have taken refuge.

The RPF have warned the French intervention forces that they intend to capture the 'clique of killers' whom the rebels say are being shielded by the French. The French say they will not tolerate any RPF incursions into the area.

But a possible showdown with the French may be the least of the RPF's problems. General Kagame and his RPF army now face the formidable task of convincing millions of displaced Hutus, many of whom participated in massacres of Tutsis, that they are welcome to return and safe from retribution.

But so far the RPF victory does not provide much optimism for reconciliation. Although about 20,000 Hutus and Tutsis have returned to Kigali, there is still an air of unease hanging over the city. Arrogant young rebel soldiers man checkpoints throughout the town. There have been reports of looting of Hutu houses by RPF troops in the capital and several incidents of abuse of Hutu men.

The RPF's success may have inadvertently recreated similar conditions to those of 1959 when the Hutus, rebelling against centuries of Tutsi domination, killed 100,000 Tutsis and drove another 200,000 into exile in Uganda. The inability of the Tutsis to go home provided the pretext for the creation of the RPF and the start of its armed struggle to return with a refugee army. The war in turn eventually led to the massacres of Tutsis over the last three months.

Already there are signs that the refugee camps outside Rwanda are being used as bases for Hutu extremist incursions into the country. Relief workers in Ngara refugee camp in Tanzania report that for the past week about 15 new bodies—supposedly those of Tutsis—are once again flowing down the Kigare river from Rwanda every day.

In an attempt to reassure the Hutus of their good intentions, the RPF has named a Hutu, Pasteur Bizimungu, as the new president of the country and has also appointed a Hutu prime minister. But many observers, including senior UN officials, think that Hutus will view them as RPF puppets. 'The only way the RPF can convince the Hutus to return is to stop all military action, allow the safe zone to remain intact and avoid the kind of incident like the mortar attack on Goma,' said one UN official.

The Refugee Camps Create a Humanitarian and Political Crisis

Doctors Without Borders

In the following viewpoint, a humanitarian aid organization reports on conditions in the refugee camps following the genocide and the takeover of Rwanda by Tutsi-led forces. According to the author, the camps are largely controlled by government officials from the former Hutu government, and many of those responsible for the genocide operate freely in the camps. Hutu officials spread frightening propaganda about the Tutsi government to discourage Hutus from returning and also deny the genocide and emphasize Hutu victimization. The author concludes that humanitarian activity in the camp is morally compromised and suggests that conditions in the camps may pose long-term political dangers to stability in Rwanda. Doctors Without Borders is an international humanitarian organization that provides emergency medical relief to those affected by disasters, conflicts, and epidemics.

The repatriation of about two million Rwandan Hutu refugees from countries neighboring Rwanda has come to a virtual standstill [in 1995]. Parts of the Rwandan Government and the Rwandan population consider the refugee camps to be a clear threat to their security. Fear of reprisal killings, mass arbitrary arrests, reports about grossly overcrowded prisons, the lack of an effective judicial system and the control exercised by their leaders over the camps have prevented many refugees and internally displaced people (the displaced) from returning home.

One year after the genocide in Rwanda in which Hutu extremists systematically slaughtered between 500,000 and one million Tutsi and moderate Hutus, there is still no justice for the victims and their families. The killers continue to go unpunished and some of those responsible for the genocide walk freely in the Rwandan refugee camps in Tanzania and Zaire, controlling the camp populations and preparing for renewed attacks.

The former Rwandan Government officials have taken steps to improve the public image of the camps in order to ensure continued humanitarian assistance. However, these changes are cosmetic and in fact little has changed since November 1994, when MSF [Médecins Sans Frontières/Doctors Without Borders] said that the situation in the camps could not be sustained. On the surface, the climate in the camps has improved. Aid workers are no longer threatened, soldiers are rarely seen, and militia training no longer takes place in public. Many members of the military have left the camps and those who remain wear civilian clothes. However, the same government officials who incited the Hutu population to genocide with extremist propaganda continue to manipulate the refugees by controlling the flow of information and political discourse in the camps. They talk tirelessly about the victimization of the Hutu people.

The Refugee Crisis Drags On

Criminal trials, national or international, have yet to take place. Despite their pledges, the international community has failed to give adequate support to rebuilding Rwanda's judicial system which continues to be severely hampered by a lack of human and material resources. Countries in which alleged perpetrators of the genocide reside have failed to bring them to justice. The

Deputy Prosecutor of the International Tribunal for Rwanda, created in November 1994, has announced that he expected the first indictment to be handed down at the beginning of 1996.

Rwanda lacks the resources either to house its detainees properly or try them effectively. Nevertheless, mass arrests of alleged perpetrators of the genocide continue. Roughly 49,000 people are detained in overcrowded prisons and lock-ups. For example, Gitarama prison, which was designed for 400 prisoners in reasonable conditions, now holds nearly 7,000. The absence of basic sanitary and hygienic conditions has led to alarmingly high mortality rates. The average rate for the first three months of 1995 was 9.6/10,000 per day whereas 2/10,000 per day is already considered a full-scale emergency.

At the end of 1994, the Rwandan Government declared that the camps for the internally displaced in southern Rwanda, believed to harbor Hutu militia, must be closed. By April 1995, an estimated 250,000 out of the original 380,000 displaced remained in the camps. Operation Retour, agreed between the Rwandan Government, UNAMIR [United Nations Assistance Mission in Rwanda] and UNREO [United Nations Rwanda Emergency Office], failed to convince the vast majority of the displaced to return voluntarily to their home communes.

On 22 April 1995, thousands of displaced in Kibeho were massacred by the RPA [Rwanda Patriotic Army] during the forced closure of the camp. UNAMIR failed to protect the victims.

The Rwandan refugee camps in Zaire, Tanzania and Burundi cannot be sustained in the long term. Those suspected of genocide who still reside in the camps and elsewhere should be arrested and tried. The remaining refugees should be free to decide whether to return to Rwanda.

This report looks at factors from both inside and outside Rwanda which have led to the virtual standstill in repatriation. One year after the mass exodus from Rwanda there are still no lasting solutions for the regional refugee crisis. This report also addresses the issue of impunity, as MSF has always maintained

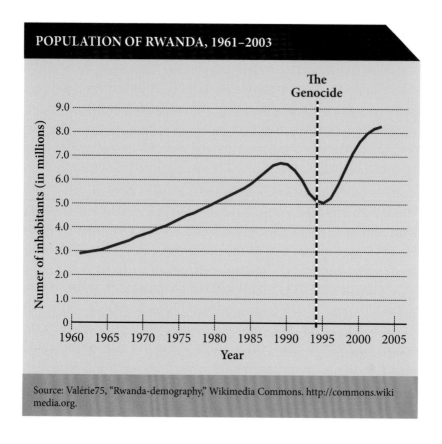

POPULATION OF RWANDA, 1961–2003

The Genocide

Source: Valérie75, "Rwanda-demography," Wikimedia Commons. http://commons.wiki media.org.

that it should be a priority that those responsible for the genocide be brought to justice without delay, and that the refugee camps in which MSF provides humanitarian relief should not be given the de facto status of safe havens for those who committed crimes against humanity. Further this report reflects on the moral dilemma faced by MSF and many other aid agencies working in camps in which killers walk freely and where preparations are made for a military intervention into Rwanda aimed at further massacres of the Tutsi population.

Improvements in humanitarian aid and the comparable calm in the camps belie the fact that those who instigated, prepared, or committed acts of genocide and serious violations of international humanitarian law continue to control the camps and manipulate the population for their own political ends. It is widely reported that they are rearming for a renewed attack. Continued impunity in the refugee camps, in Rwanda and in UN Member States harboring the killers, coupled together with the rearmament of the former Rwandan Armed Forces and militia, will only lead to a further cycle of violence. This cycle must be broken. . . .

MSF Expresses Concerns

In November 1994, MSF published its report *Breaking the Cycle*. In this report, MSF compiled evidence of its concerns that: the situation in the refugee camps could not be sustained and that for MSF to continue to give humanitarian relief in these circumstances presented a moral dilemma; refugees alleged of having participated in the genocide walk around freely in the camps. MSF reiterated that there was also growing evidence that the refugee camps were becoming training bases for members of the militia and the former Rwandan armed forces and that military training occurred openly.

Consequently, MSF called on the relevant UN bodies and individual member states to take all necessary measures to ensure: that refugees receive adequate protection and do not have to live in fear for their lives, to which end an international police force and human rights monitors should be dispatched to the camps. Further MSF recommended that refugee registration should take place as soon as possible; that the distribution of food should not be controlled by camp leaders and that refugees be guaranteed equal access to humanitarian aid; that the militia and military be separated from the refugees. Moreover all members of the military and militia should be disarmed; all those suspected of genocide who currently walk freely in the camps should be brought to justice, either by states on whose territory these killers reside or by the then newly established International Tribunal.

At that time, many other humanitarian relief agencies, outraged that they were becoming unwilling accomplices to the perpetrators of the genocide, threatened to pull out. . . .

Camp Leaders Undermine Humanitarian Aid Efforts

In the autumn of 1994, refugees were regularly subjected to violence and sometimes killed publicly because of their wish to return to Rwanda. Such incidents, together with meetings led by camp leaders to urge the refugees not to return effectively acted to hold the population hostage. Intent on disproving allegations that this was the case, the leaders neither openly discouraged nor resorted to physical violence themselves. Their use of speeches inciting ethnic hatred and extremist propaganda was sufficiently successful and, in fact, they could even tell the refugees that they were free to return. This new policy fit perfectly into the designed improved image of the camp leadership.

The Rwandan Refugees in Goma, Zaire

During the first three months of 1995, there was a small, but constant flow of refugees repatriating to Rwanda in convoys organized by UNHCR [the United Nations High Commissioner for Refugees]. However, since April, repatriation has come to a virtual standstill. Intent on disproving allegations that they were holding the population hostage, the Hutu leaders in the camps officially told the refugees that they were free to return. However, repatriation rapidly declined as refugees became more convinced that it was too dangerous to go back to Rwanda, a conviction that was reinforced by the anti-RPA propaganda and hate campaign carried out by camp leaders and the deteriorating situation in Rwanda. Early July, repatriation has started again, amounting to about 50 to 100 refugees per week.

In the immediate aftermath of the cholera and dysentery epidemics [of July and August, 1994], lawlessness prevailed. Assassinations of supposed RPF [Rwandan Patriotic Front] spies were reported and allegations of open military training were common. Within days of crossing the border, the refugees began to organize themselves according to the same state administrative structures which had existed in Rwanda. In the chaos brought

Soldiers from the defeated Hutu-controlled Rwandan army walk freely through the Kibumba refugee camp in Zaire in August 1994. Médecins Sans Frontières-Belgium pulled out of this camp in February 1995 because of the excessive influence of Hutu militia members. © Mike Goldwater/Alamy.

about by the sheer numbers, UNHCR and relief agencies were forced to rely on those who presented themselves as leaders among a disoriented and severely traumatized population. Initially, many who had manipulated the population to commit genocide in Rwanda were recognized in the camps by UNHCR and NGOs [nongovernmental organizations] as legitimate, or at least desperately needed, representatives of the massive refugee population.

On 3 November 1994, 16 international NGOs, including MSF, issued a joint press release stating that working conditions in the camps had become unacceptably dangerous and they would be forced to withdraw unless there was immediate action to improve security. The statement declared that refugees wishing to return home were virtually held hostage by the camp leaders. The NGOs demanded that those responsible for inciting violence and disrupting the delivery of humanitarian aid should be separated from the other refugees and that all weapons should be removed from the camps. Furthermore, adequate protection for refugees needed to be guaranteed in order for them to feel free to return home or remain in the camp without fearing for their lives.

Four days later, MSF-France announced its decision to pull out of the camps in Zaire and Tanzania, stating that the continued diversion of humanitarian aid by the same leaders who orchestrated the genocide, the lack of effective international action regarding impunity, the fact that the refugee population was being held hostage, presented a situation contradictory with the principles of humanitarian assistance. Later that month, Care-Canada pulled out of Katale camp following death threats. MSF-Belgium and -Holland decided to continue working in the camps while at the same time continuously and publicly advocating for an end to impunity and improvements in the security situation for the refugees.

Camp Leaders Modify Their Approach

After the criticism of the international aid community the self-proclaimed government-in-exile instituted a series of 'reforms' in order to ensure continued humanitarian assistance and to improve the public image of the camps by targeting their 'constituency', advance 'democracy', and promote 'legitimate' leaders to pursue the possibility of political negotiations with the government in Kigali.

The Commission Sociale was formed, comprising 15 principal members, the majority of whom identify themselves as either former government ministers or pro-MRND [National Revolutionary Movement for Development party] politicians, to act as an informal link between the self-proclaimed government-in-exile, international bodies, and the refugees in North Kivu. The Commission Sociale played an ill-defined but critical role in carrying out a concerted campaign to revamp the public image of the camps. During the months that followed, elections were held, camp security structures were re-organized, and countless civic organizations were founded.

However, the new strategy of the camp leaders also appeared to be "aimed at causing unrest inside Rwanda to undermine the new government and convince refugees that it was too dangerous to return".

MSF therefore maintains that these changes are cosmetic and that little has in fact changed since November 1994. On the surface, the climate in the camps has improved. Aid workers are no longer threatened, soldiers are rarely seen, and militia training no longer takes place in public. Many members of the military have left the camps and those who remain wear civilian clothes.

Following the failure of UN Secretary-General Boutros Boutros Ghali's proposal for an international peacekeeping force, the deployment of 1,500 Zairian troops to the camps has improved the security of refugees on UNHCR repatriation convoys and of non-governmental organizations (NGOs) operating in the camps. While the camps now operate smoothly and relative calm prevails, field officials of NGOs and of the UN High Commissioner for Refugees (UNHCR) may be lulled into a false sense of complacency.

Refugee registration process was poorly planned and fraught with fraud. MSF-Belgium's efforts to control systematic cheating and intimidation by militia members in Kibumba led to expatriate staff being threatened. Declaring this militia control of the camp unacceptable, MSF-Belgium pulled out of Kibumba on 8 February 1995. In response to the high level of fraud, UNHCR spent two months conducting registration card verification before finally arriving at more or less accurate population figures. In the Tanzanian refugee camp Ngara, UNHCR nullified the registration after widespread fraud. The registration will be re-done in July/August 1995.

Distribution of Food Aid Has Improved

Commonly referred to as 'camp leaders', the representatives of the refugees were responsible for food distribution to their segment of the population. They exerted blatant control over the camps in the form of routine violence, threats, and massive diversion of food aid.

Food is now distributed directly to families or cellules (groups) in most camps. The level of diversion has decreased and the control of the camp leaders over humanitarian aid has largely diminished. However, the delay in registration resulted in the diversion of thousands of tons of food aid. Much of it was alleged to have been stockpiled for former Rwandan soldiers. Food basket monitors now oversee the equitable distribution of aid. Security incidents no longer surround the distribution of food, except when there is little food to distribute.

In February 1995, the World Food Program (WFP) found itself falling short of funds to feed the three million refugees, returnees, and displaced in the Great Lakes region. Rations were reduced to as little as 503 kcal per day, resulting in daily scenes of chaos, protests and threats at the distribution sites. On 24 March 1995, MSF issued a public statement together with 32 other humanitarian organizations in the region, urging the international community to act swiftly to end the food shortage. The appeal emphasized the fact that the food shortage threatened regional stability. MSF maintains that withholding food would not, as some donor countries apparently believed, encourage repatriation. However, MSF also believes it is very serious that the international community still feeds soldiers and militia who are alleged to have been implicated in the genocide.

Humanitarian aid should not be used to bring about political solutions. A month later, WFP reached 70% of the $385 million needed for 1995. Since then, rations have steadily increased.

Questionable Elections Establish a New Security Structure

In spite of 'democratic reforms' former politicians implicated in the genocide continue to dominate the political life of the camps. The fact that many refugees say they were never told of any elections further calls into question the nature of these 'reforms'.

It is sure that some elections took place in many of the camps in Eastern Zaire in December 1994 and the early months of 1995. The Commission Sociale, eager to promote the appearance of grassroots democracy, said that the refugees called for elections themselves. These provided an opportunity to elect legitimate representatives among the refugee population while at the same time replacing leaders who may not have conformed to the government-in-exile's larger political objectives. However, elections were not held in every prefecture and the replacement of camp leaders was very selective. In practice, the elections appear to have been orchestrated by former government officials.

In Katale camp, for example, the former mayor of Greater Kigali, best known for his statement in an interview with the *New York Times* that the killings in Rwanda did not constitute genocide because some Tutsi had survived, presided over mid-January elections in Ruhengeri prefecture part of the camp. Accompanied by the former mayor of Ruhengeri, he conducted a campaign to influence the refugees which of the two candidates to vote for (*sensibilisation de la population*) before, during, and after the elections. Later, the two candidates themselves spoke only briefly. Refugees maintained that they were free to vote for the candidate of their choice.

In December 1994, as part of its public image campaign, the Commission Sociale restructured the camps into quartiers (districts), sous-quartiers (sub-districts), cellules (neighborhoods) and nyumba kumi (groups of ten houses), each with their own representative, allegedly duly elected. The goal was twofold: to ensure that the refugees could properly defend themselves against 'RPA infiltrators'; and to assert control over a security situation which threatened continued humanitarian assistance. A dual power structure was imposed so that camp leaders now have responsibility according both to where they currently live in the camps and to their commune of origin in Rwanda. Neighborhood representatives, in charge of security, serve to reinforce the power of the camp president. At the same time they rival the power of the administrative representatives.

This highly centralized security structure is identical to that which was perfected in Rwanda prior to the genocide. According to African Rights [organization], a September 1991 Ministry of Defense memorandum entitled "Auto-défense de la population" envisaged at least one armed man for every ten households. This 'home guard' project foreshadowed the creation of the militia throughout the country under the control of senior military officials. During the genocide, Interahamwe [militia] knew exactly who lived in which house. They were therefore able to carry out the killings literally door by door. The localized command structure in the camps is based on this same model.

A Civil Society Disguises Extremism

The final step towards improving the public image of the camps and pushing for political negotiations was the creation of a civil society (as opposed to overt military control) and a new political party. The Commission Sociale was instrumental in restructuring the camps and supporting the expansion of the camp leadership. It has now given way to the Société Civile which purports to represent a broad spectrum of society. The Commission Sociale is a member of the Société Civile and now distances itself from the self-proclaimed government-in-exile. The latter is equally ambiguous about its links with former Rwandan Government authorities.

Founded on 14 January 1995, six months after the refugees arrived in Goma, the Société Civile currently boasts 92 affiliated non-profit-making organizations such as: l'Association des journalistes rwandais en exil, le Cercle des intellectuels, l'Association pour la promotion féminine et la réhabilitation de la famille rwandaise, and l'Association des juristes pour les droits de l'homme. Most were founded by members of Rwanda's well-educated elite, the MRND, and of the extremist media that functioned in Rwanda before the genocide. Some receive substantial funding from abroad. The primary goal of the Société Civile is to act as the representative of the refugee population in any negotiations for a political settlement with the government in Kigali.

On 3 April 1995, a group of refugees in Mugunga formed the Rally for Democracy and the Return to Rwanda (RDR), a new political party which also denies any formal link with the self-proclaimed government-in-exile. Like the Société Civile, the leaders of the RDR portray themselves as moderates. Nevertheless, they have emerged from the same ideological background as the extremists, they justify the genocide and paint themselves as victims. They circulate a list of all human rights abuses in Rwanda since October 1990 when the RPF first invaded the country and claim to give a "truthful accounting of the facts" surrounding the death of President Habyarimana; this is followed by a long list of what they consider to be prerequisites for peace. The RDR states that if they fail to attain their political objectives, they will resort to "military action as a final option". On 4 April 1995, 13 senior commanders of the former Rwandan Armed Forces (ex-FAR) issued a public statement pledging their support for the RDR. The Zairian authorities have forbidden the RDR to hold public demonstrations and activities. As a result, the party carries out its activities clandestine.

While some believe that these recent political developments herald the dawning of a new era, the host of new leaders appears to have emerged from the same Hutu extremist ideological position. The expansion of the camp leadership, the creation of the Société Civile and a new 'independent' political party have not broadened the political spectrum. Indeed, they have served to further the monopoly of extremism. In the highly polarized political climate of the camps, there is virtually no room for moderate voices to be heard.

A Perpetrator of Genocide in Rwanda Is Sentenced by International Law

International Criminal Tribunal for Rwanda

The International Criminal Tribunal for Rwanda (ICTR) is an international court established by the United Nations in 1994 to try those responsible for the Rwandan genocide. In the following viewpoint, ICTR reports on the sentencing of Jean-Paul Akayesu, former bourgmestre *(the highest regional position) of the Taba commune in Rwanda. The court found Akayesu guilty of crimes against humanity, genocide, murder, and rape, and sentenced him to life imprisonment. Akayesu argued that he had tried to oppose the genocide in part, and he had been a minor official and should be treated leniently. However, the court found that his active participation in murder and rape, and his encouragement of the genocide, outweighed the mitigating circumstances.*

Precisely one month after finding him guilty on nine of the fifteen charges in his indictment, Trial Chamber I of the ICTR [International Criminal Tribunal for Rwanda], sitting in Arusha [Tanzania] today, sentenced Jean-Paul Akayesu, former Bourgmestre of the Taba Commune in Rwanda.

The Trial Chamber, made up of Judge Laïty Kama, Presiding, and Judges Lennart Aspegren and Navanethem Pillay, decided to follow the principle of multiple sentences, in other words, to give a penalty on each of the counts for which it found Akayesu guilty. Consequently, it decided:

Count 1: Genocide—to life imprisonment;

Count 3: Crime against humanity (extermination)—to life imprisonment;

Count 4: Direct and Public incitement to commit genocide—to life imprisonment;

Count 5: Crime against humanity (murder)—to 15 years imprisonment;

Count 7: Crime against humanity (murder)—to 15 years imprisonment;

Count 9: Crime against humanity (murder)—to 15 years imprisonment;

Count 11: Crime against humanity (torture)—to 10 years imprisonment;

Count 13: Crime against humanity (rape)—to 15 years imprisonment;

Count 14: Crime against humanity (other inhumane acts)—to 10 years imprisonment.

As the Trial Chamber had passed concurrent sentences, Akayesu will serve a single sentence of life imprisonment.

Determination of the Sentence of Akayesu

The Trial Chamber established, as it did in its first judgement, in the case of The Prosecutor versus [former Rwandan prime minister] Jean Kambanda, that neither the Statute of the Tribunal, nor its Rules of Procedure and Evidence, specify a scale of penalties applicable for each of the offences falling within the jurisdiction of the ICTR, in other words, genocide, crimes against humanity and violations of Article 3 common to the Geneva Conventions and their Additional Protocol II. The Statute provides that the Trial Chamber, in determining prison terms, shall have recourse to the general scale of prison sentences applied by the courts of Rwanda. However, the Trial Chamber again considered that any reference to the said scale was indicative and therefore not binding. Consequently, while referring as much as possible to the general scale of prison sentences applied by Rwandan courts, the Trial Chamber considered its sovereignty to judge paramount, considering the circumstances of the case and various factors such as mitigating circumstances, aggravating circumstances and the individual situation of the accused.

The Trial Chamber also observed that neither the Statute nor the Rules of Procedure determine a specific penalty for each of the three crimes mentioned above, falling within the jurisdiction of the Tribunal, and that the Statute does not indicate any hierarchical relationship between them, as the applicable penalty is theoretically the same for each of them: a prison sentence which may extend up to life imprisonment. The Trial Chamber therefore examined the question whether there was a hierarchical relationship between these crimes and concluded that it was difficult to establish any difference between the gravity of the crime of genocide and of crimes against humanity respectively. Both crimes against humanity, already punished by the Nuremberg and Tokyo Tribunals [which punished crimes committed by Nazi Germany and Japan during World War II], and genocide, a crime of which the actual concept was defined only later, are crimes which particularly shock the conscience of humanity. It did however indicate that it considers genocide to be the "crime of crimes".

The Prosecutor's Submissions on the Sentence

In her submission given on 28 September 1998, the Prosecutor focused on the extreme gravity of the crimes committed by Akayesu, arguing that these crimes deserved appropriate pun-

UN security personnel escort Jean-Paul Akayesu to his trial at the International Criminal Tribunal for Rwanda in Arusha, Tanzania, on January 9, 1997. Akayesu was sentenced to life imprisonment after the court found him guilty of genocide and related crimes. © AP Images/ Sayyid Azim.

ishment and that the Trial Chamber should assess the individual role of the accused in the crimes as well as the specific circumstances. As the Prosecutor saw it, Akayesu occupied a position of authority and had the duty to protect the population and ensure its security, but he betrayed the people's trust, took advantage of his powers in order to commit crimes and made use of the communal police in committing the crimes; he was actuated by the intention to commit genocide and planned his acts accordingly, acting with intent. His criminal behaviour was sustained and systematic and lasted approximately three months, becoming progressively more intensive. Furthermore, the Prosecutor submitted that on the basis of the information she possessed, there

and that he made efforts to impede them and finally, the Prosecutor accepted that Akayesu has no prior criminal conviction.

Regarding the aggravating factors: Akayesu consciously chose to participate in the systematic killings that took place in Taba and, without being a very high official in the Government, his position as Bourgmestre made him the highest Governmental authority in Taba and as such, he was entrusted with the protection of the population and he betrayed this trust. He publicly incited killings in Taba. He also ordered and participated in the murder of a number of people, some of whom were killed in his presence. He also condoned and, by his presence and actions, encouraged the rape of many women at the communal offices.

The Trial Chamber having considered all the aspects involved and having weighed the mitigating factors in relation to the aggravating factors in the case, found that the aggravating factors far outweighed the mitigating factors, all the more so in light of the fact that Akayesu consciously chose to participate in the genocide.

CHAPTER 2

Controversies Surrounding the Rwandan Genocide

Chapter Exercises

Country of Asylum	1993	1994	1995	1996	1997	1998	1999
RWANDAN REFUGEE POPULATIONS IN NEIGHBORING COUNTRIES, 1993–1999							
Burundi	245,500	278,100	153,000	720	2,000	2,000	1,300
DR Congo (ex-Zaire)	53,500	1,252,800	1,100,600	423,600	37,000	35,000	33,000
Tanzania	51,900	626,200	548,000	20,000	410	4,800	20,100
Uganda	97,000	97,000	6,500	11,200	12,200	7,500	8,000
Total	447,900	2,254,100	1,808,100	455,520	51,610	49,300	62,400

Source: United Nations High Commissioner for Refugees, "The State of the World's Refugees 2000: Fifty Years of Humanitarian Action," January 1, 2000, p. 250. www.unhcr.org.

1. Analyze the Chart

Question 1: How many Rwandan refugees were residing in Rwanda's neighboring countries in 1993 before the genocide began? How did the Rwandan refugee population in these countries change in 1994—the year of the genocide? How did it change after the genocide?

Question 2: What could account for the population of refugees living outside of Rwanda before the genocide began? Do you think the refugees were mostly Hutu or Tutsi?

Question 3: Which country hosted the most Rwandan refugees before 1994? How did this change in 1994 and the years after? What could account for this change?

2. Writing Prompt

Write an editorial from the perspective of either a Tutsi or a Hutu and argue why the events in early 1994 were or were not a genocide in your point of view. Use evidence and facts from the readings in this chapter to support your argument.

3. Group Activity

Form two groups for a debate. One group will adopt the position that the Rwandan genocide could have been prevented or considerably restrained had the United States or the United Nations sent troops when the genocide began. The other group will argue that Western intervention could not have prevented the atrocities committed in Rwanda in 1994. Gather information from the viewpoints in this volume to support your argument.

There Was No Genocide of Tutsis in Rwanda

David Peterson and Edward S. Herman

The authors of the following viewpoint argue that there was no genocide of Tutsis by Hutus. Instead, they argue, most of the killings in Rwanda were perpetrated by the Rwandan Patriotic Front (RPF)—the Tutsi revolutionaries—who assassinated President Juvénal Habyarimana and then murdered Hutus as they took over the country. The authors say that Western powers supported the RPF and its leader, Paul Kagame, and helped him take over the country. They conclude that the United States and Western powers have covered up the violence by the RPF and have substituted a false story of genocide committed by Hutus. David Peterson is a journalist and researcher based in Chicago, and Edward S. Herman is professor emeritus of finance at the Wharton School of the University of Pennsylvania.

Elsewhere we have written that the breakup of Yugoslavia "may have been the most misrepresented series of major events over the past twenty years." But the far bloodier and more destructive invasions, insurgencies, and civil wars that have ravaged several countries in the Great Lakes region of Central Af-

David Peterson and Edward S. Herman, "Rwanda and the Democratic Republic of Congo in the Propaganda System," *Monthly Review*, vol. 62, no. 1, May 2010. Copyright © 2010 Monthly Review. Reproduced by permission.

rica over the same years may have been subjected to even greater misrepresentation.

To a remarkable degree, all major sectors of the Western establishment swallowed a propaganda line on Rwanda that turned perpetrator and victim upside-down. In the much-cited 1999 study, *Leave None to Tell the Story: Genocide in Rwanda*, on behalf of Human Rights Watch and the International Federation of Human Rights in Paris, [historian and human rights activist] Alison Des Forges writes that "By late March 1994, Hutu Power leaders were determined to slaughter massive numbers of Tutsi and Hutu opposed to [Hutu President Juvénal] Habyarimana," and that on April 6, 1994, with the assassination of Habyarimana, "[a] small group of his close associates . . . decided to execute the planned extermination."

Although "responsibility for killing Habyarimana is a serious issue," writes Des Forges, it pales in comparison to "responsibility for the genocide. We know little about who assassinated Habyarimana." This is a false statement, as we show in detail below. "We know more about who used the assassination as the pretext to begin a slaughter that had been planned for months" is true enough, but in exactly the opposite sense reported by Des Forges.

During testimony at a major trial of four Hutu former military officers before the International Criminal Tribunal for Rwanda (ICTR), Des Forges acknowledged that by April 1992 (i.e., a full twenty-four months before "The Genocide" is alleged to have been perpetrated), the "government in charge of Rwanda [had become] a multiparty government, including Tutsi representatives, and it is for that reason alone that it is impossible to conclude that there was planning of a genocide by that government."

Although Des Forges tried to salvage the Hutu conspiracy model, alleging plans by individual Hutu members of the coalition government to use their "official powers" to carry out a preplanned genocide, this model disintegrated on cross-examination. Des Forges could not explain how Hutu "individuals" used these "powers" without the knowledge of their Tutsi and Rwandan Patriotic Front (RPF) associates. Furthermore, she was forced to admit that pro-RPF ministers were in cahoots with the RPF and its plans for war (which we describe below), and that after the Habyarimana assassination, the RPF did not simply respond in self-defense to a Hutu-organized killing spree, but initiated its own killing spree. In other words, while the Hutu members of Rwanda's power-sharing government would have had great difficulty organizing a genocide against the Tutsi, the Tutsi-led RPF was well-positioned to paralyze any government response to plans it had developed—and that were implemented—to avoid the threat of a free election the RPF was destined to lose, to assassinate the Hutu president, and to take over the country by military force. Yet Des Forges's dramatic concessions before the ICTR never turned up in the Western media, and in her public statements thereafter she continued to repeat the official propaganda line about a Hutu conspiracy to commit genocide, right up to the very end.

RPF Actions Constituted Aggression

To accept the standard model of "The Genocide," one must ignore the large-scale killing and ethnic cleansing of Hutus by the RPF long before the April–July 1994 period, which began when Ugandan forces invaded Rwanda under President (and dictator) Yoweri Museveni on October 1, 1990. At its inception, the RPF was a wing of the Ugandan army, the RPF's leader, Paul Kagame, having served as director of Ugandan military intelligence in the 1980s. The Ugandan invasion and resultant combat were not a "civil war," but rather a clear case of *aggression*. However, the invasion led to no reprimand or cessation of support by the United States or Britain—and, in contrast to Iraq's invasion of Kuwait just two months before, which was countered in the Security Council by a same-day demand that Iraq withdraw its forces immediately—the Council took no action on the Ugandan invasion of Rwanda until March 1993. It did not even authorize an observer mission (UNOMUR) until late June 1993, the RPF by then having occupied much of northern Rwanda and driven out several hundred thousand Hutu farmers.

It is clear that Museveni and the RPF were perceived as serving U.S. interests, and that the government of President Habyarimana was targeted for ouster. UN Security Council inaction flowed from this political bias. In his assessment of the years he spent representing U.S. interests in Africa, former Assistant Secretary of State Herman Cohen raised the question of why, as of October 1, 1990, the "first day of the crisis," as he calls it, "did [the United States] automatically exclude the policy option of informing Ugandan President Museveni that the invasion of Rwanda by uniformed members of the Ugandan army was totally unacceptable, and that the continuation of good relations between the United States and Uganda would depend on his getting the RPF back across the border?" This question is naïve but revealing—the answer, like that to the question of why the United States lobbied for the withdrawal of UN forces from Rwanda as "The Genocide" was getting under way in April 1994, is that the Ugandan army and RPF were doing what the United States wanted done in Rwanda.

The United States and its allies worked hard in the early 1990s to weaken the Rwandan government, forcing the abandonment of many of the economic and social gains from the social revolution of 1959, thereby making the Habyarimana government less popular, and helping to reinforce the Tutsi minority's economic power. Eventually, the RPF was able to achieve a legal military presence inside Rwanda, thanks to a series of ceasefires and other agreements. These agreements led to the Arusha Peace Accords of August 1993, pressed upon the Rwandan government by the United States and its allies, called for the "integration" of the armed forces of Rwanda and the RPF, and for a "transitional," power-sharing government until national elections could be held in 1995. These Peace Accords positioned the RPF for its bloody

Who Assassinated Rwandan President Juvénal Habyarimana?

Who killed [President Juvénal] Habyarimana is a critical question, but one that current evidence cannot definitively answer. There are two principal hypotheses: one blames the Hutu hardliners who subsequently took over and orchestrated the genocide, and the other blames the RPF [Tutsi rebel group] who subsequently launched an offensive and ultimately won the civil war. There are problems with both theories, but the current balance of evidence suggests that the RPF was responsible.

The thinking behind the first theory is that the hardliners were angry about Habyarimana's concessions to the RPF in the Arusha Accords [of 1993 ending the civil war]. Rather than share power, the hardliners would have decided to sacrifice the president and destroy the Tutsi threat once and for all. The theory has a number of problems, but two stand out. First, the assassination was a terrible blow to the hardliners. Not only did the assassination kill key players in the hardliners' camp—presumably those who would have planned the genocide had it been planned before April 6, 1994—but other key officials were also out of the country, including the defense minister and the chief of military intelligence. The timing for the hardliners, in short, was quite poor. Second, since the geno-

overthrow of a relatively democratic coalition government, and the takeover of the Rwandan state by a minority dictatorship.

As we have already suggested, the established perpetrator-victim line requires suppression of the crucial fact that the April 6 shooting-down of the government jet returning Rwanda President Juvénal Habyarimana and Burundi President Cyprian Ntaryamira to Kigali, that killed everyone onboard, was carried out by RPF commandos (as discussed below), and had been regarded by RPF planners as an essential first strike in its final assault on the government. Although the mass killings *followed* cide, neither the RPF nor the well-funded International Criminal Tribunal for Rwanda [ICTR] has produced concrete evidence to implicate the hardliners in the assassination. Generating such evidence is strongly in the interest of both parties.

The thinking behind the second theory is that the Tutsi rebels would have desired a clean military victory rather than a negotiated political settlement. Fed up with the hardliners' obstacles to implementing the Arusha Accords and unsure of their popular support, under this theory the RPF opted for a lightning strike and quick offensive. There is evidence to support the theory. To date, the most comprehensive investigation of the assassination—a six-year French magistrate inquiry—concluded that the RPF was responsible for the assassination. (The magistrate investigated because the plane's two pilots, who also were killed, were French.) Several RPF dissidents also blame the rebel leadership, in particular former rebel leader Paul Kagame, for planning and ordering the assassination. The main problem with the theory is that the assassination triggered the genocide. If the theory is correct, then the RPF leadership must have miscalculated their ability to win the war quickly, the impact of the president's assassination, or the depravity of their opponents—or some combination of the three.

Scott Straus, "Genocide at the National and Regional Levels," in The Order of Genocide: Race, Power, and War in Rwanda. *Ithaca, NY: Cornell University Press, 2006, pp. 44–45.*

this assassination, with the RPF rapidly defeating any military resistance by the successor to Habyarimana's coalition government and establishing its rule in Rwanda, these prime *génocidaires* were, and still are today, portrayed as heroic defenders of Rwanda's national unity against Hutu "extremists" and the *Interahamwe* militia, who were the RPF's actual victims.

Acceptance of this line also requires the suppression of a key verdict in a December 2008 Judgment by the ICTR. This seven-and-a-half year trial of four former high-ranking Hutu members of the Rwanda military produced an acquittal of all four defendants on the Tribunal's most serious charge: participation in a conspiracy to commit genocide against the country's Tutsi minority. To the contrary, the court ruled unanimously that the evidence was "consistent with preparations for a political or military power struggle and measures adopted in the context of an on-going war with the RPF that were used for other purposes from 6 April 1994."

The RPF Had U.S. Support

Of course, it was the RPF that had been organized to carry out a "military power struggle" against Rwanda's Hutu majority for several years prior to April 1994; and with its Tutsi base a numerical minority in the country (at most 15 percent overall), the RPF recognized that they would suffer an almost certain defeat in the free elections called for by the Arusha Accords. But the fact that the RPF itself conspired to assassinate Habyarimana and to carry out subsequent mass killings remains entirely beyond the grasp of the ICTR. Although it has failed to convict a single Hutu of conspiracy to commit genocide, the ICTR has never once entertained the question of an RPF conspiracy—despite the RPF's rapid overthrow of the Hutu government and capture of the Rwandan state. This, we believe, flows from U.S. and allied support of the RPF, reflected in media coverage, humanitarian intellectuals' and NGO [nongovernmental organization] activism, as well as the ICTR's jurisprudence. Like the International Criminal Tribunal for the Former Yugoslavia (ICTY), the ICTR was a creation of the Security Council. Both have served Western, and notably U.S., purposes throughout their remit, but the ICTR has acted far more uncompromisingly than the ICTY—which makes this particular Judgment even more striking and important.

Paul Kagame and the RPF were creatures of U.S. power from their origins in Uganda in the 1980s. Allan Stam, a Rwanda scholar who once served with the U.S. Army Special Forces, notes that Kagame "had spent some time at Fort Leavenworth . . . not too far before the 1994 genocide." Fort Leavenworth is the U.S.

Army's "commander general staff college . . . where rising stars of the U.S. military and other places go to get training as they are on track to become generals. The training that they get there is on planning large scale operations. It's not planning small-scale logistic things. It's not tactics. It's about how do you plan an invasion. And apparently [Kagame] did very well."

By 1994, Kagame's RPF possessed, in addition to the necessary manpower and material, a sophisticated plan for seizing power in Rwanda that, in its final execution, Stam says, "looks staggeringly like the United States' invasion of Iraq in 1991." Stam adds that the RPF launched its final assault on the Rwandan government almost immediately after the assassination of Habyarimana, within 60 to 120 minutes of the shooting-down of his jet, with "50,000 [RPF] soldiers mov[ing] into action on two fronts, in a coordinated fashion"—clearly "a plan that was not worked out on the back of an envelope."

So the Hutu conspiracy model, still at the center of establishment belief even if implicitly rejected by the ICTR, suffers from the RPF-Kagame locus of responsibility for the triggering event (the shoot-down of Habyarimana's jet during its approach to Kigali airport) and the incredible speed and coordinated nature of the RPF's military response, which again suggest detailed planning, and a different set of conspirators.

But there is also the fact that the alleged Hutu perpetrators of "The Genocide" were the ones *driven from power*, with several million Hutus sent fleeing from Rwanda by July 4, the date by which the RPF had taken Kigali. We also see that, before the end of July, Washington withdrew diplomatic recognition from the ousted government and awarded it to the RPF—the "entity that exercises effective control in Rwanda," a State Department spokesman explained. And we see that, at the same time, Washington began dispatching U.S. troops and large-scale aid to Kigali, after having lobbied and voted at the Security Council on April 21 for a withdrawal of virtually all UN troops, over the objections of Rwanda's ambassador, positively facilitating both the slaughters and the RPF's conquest of power. If the established narrative about "who used the assassination as a pretext" were true, then Rwanda would be the first case in history in which a minority population, suffering destruction at the hands of its tormentors, drove its tormentors from power and assumed control of a country, all in the span of less than one hundred days. We find this incredible in the extreme.

Research Incriminating the RPF Is Suppressed

So does a body of important but suppressed research. An investigation in July and August 1994, sponsored by the UN High Commissioner for Refugees (UNHCR) to document Hutu massacres of Tutsis, found instead massacres of Hutu civilians in RPF-controlled areas of Rwanda on the order of 25,000–45,000. This finding led the UNHCR to take the extraordinary step of blocking Hutu refugees from returning to Rwanda in order to protect them. Prepared by [American consultant] Robert Gersony, the report, covered in the *New York Times*, "concluded that

On May 26, 1994, a Rwandan Patriotic Front soldier investigates the site of the plane crash in which Rwandan president Juvénal Habyarimana was killed the previous month. © Scott Peterson/Liaison/Getty Images.

there was 'an unmistakable pattern of killings and persecutions' by soldiers of the [RPF] . . . 'aimed at Hutu populations.'" But the Gersony report "set off a bitter dispute within the world organization and led the Secretary General to demand that the United Nations officials refrain from discussing it," in an effort to placate the RPF and, more importantly, its Western sponsors. Officially, the report "does not exist" at the United Nations, and Gersony was instructed never to discuss his findings (a ban he has largely respected).

A memorandum drafted in September 1994 for the eyes of Secretary of State Warren Christopher reported that the UN-HCR team "concluded that a pattern of killing had emerged" in Rwanda, the "[RPF] and Tutsi civilian surrogates [killing] 10,000 or more Hutu civilians per month, with the [RPF] accounting for 95% of the killing." This memorandum added that "the UNHCR team speculated that the purpose of the killing was a campaign of ethnic cleansing intended to clear certain areas in the south of Rwanda for Tutsi habitation. The killings also served to reduce the population of Hutu males and discouraged refugees from returning to claim their lands." The added significance of this campaign was that the south of Rwanda shares a border with northern Burundi, where a majority Tutsi population long has dwelled.

Separately, U.S. academics Christian Davenport and Allan Stam estimated that more than one million deaths occurred in Rwanda from April through July 1994, concluding that the "majority of victims were likely Hutu and not Tutsi." Initially sponsored by the ICTR, but later dropped by it, the Davenport-Stam work shows convincingly that the theaters where the killing was greatest correlated with spikes in RPF activity (i.e., with RPF "surges," in their terminology), as a series of RPF advances, particularly in the month of April 1994, created roving patterns of killing. In fact, they describe at least seven distinct "surges" by the RPF (e.g., "they surged forward from the North downward into the Northwest and middle-eastern part of the country"),

and every time, an RPF "surge" was accompanied by serious local bloodbaths. Then, in late 2009, Davenport-Stam reported
what they called the "most shocking result" of their research to
date: "The killings in the zone controlled by the FAR [i.e., the
Hutu-controlled Armed Forces of Rwanda] seemed to escalate
as the RPF moved into the country and acquired more territory.
When the RPF advanced, large-scale killings escalated. When
the RPF stopped, large-scale killings largely decreased."

With these facts, Davenport-Stam appeared to link the mass
killings of 1994 to RPF actions. This work also suggests that the
mass killings were not directed against the Tutsi population.
Moreover, a number of observers, as well as participants in the
events of 1994, claim that the great majority of deaths were Hutu,
with some estimates as high as two million.

Yet Davenport-Stam shy away from asserting the most important lesson of their work: not only that the majority of killings
took place in those theaters where the RPF "surged," but also that
the RPF was the only well-organized killing force within Rwanda
in 1994, and the only one that planned a major military offensive.
Clearly, the chief responsibility for Rwandan political violence
belonged to the RPF, and not to the ousted coalition government, the FAR, or any Hutu-related group. But Davenport-Stam
are inconsistent on the question of likely perpetrators, with their
evidence of probable RPF responsibility contradicted by asser-
tions of primary responsibility on the part of the FAR.

In short, their work does not break away from the mainstream camp, overall. However, they do acknowledge that forms
of political violence took place, other than a straightforward
Hutu "genocide" against the minority Tutsi—in itself, a rar-
ity in Western circles. As with the suppressed Gersony report,
the Davenport-Stam findings caused great dismay at the United
Nations, not to mention in Washington and Kigali. Davenport
and Stam themselves have been under attack and in retreat since
they were expelled from Rwanda in November 2003, upon first
reporting that the "majority of the victims of 1994 were of the

same ethnicity as the government in power" and have been barred from entering the country ever since. The established narrative's 800,000 or more largely Tutsi deaths resulting from a "preprogrammed genocide" committed by "Hutu Power" appears to have no basis in any facts, beyond the early claims by Kagame's RPF and its politically motivated Western sponsors and propagandists.

The RPF Was Complicit in the Jet Crash

We also know a lot more about "who assassinated Habyarimana." In one of the most important, and also suppressed, stories about "The Genocide," former ICTR investigator Michael Hourigan developed evidence as far back as 1996–1997, based on the testimony of three RPF informants who claimed "direct involvement in the 1994 fatal rocket attack upon the President's aircraft," and "specifically implicated the direct involvement of [Kagame]" and other members of the RPF. But in early 1997, when Hourigan hand-delivered his evidence to the ICTR's chief prosecutor Louise Arbour, the latter was "aggressive" and "hostile," Hourigan recounts in a 2006 affidavit, and advised him that the "investigation was at an end because in her view it was not in [the ICTR's] mandate." This decision, which "astounded" Hourigan, was rejected by former ICTR chief prosecutor Richard Goldstone, who told a Danish newspaper that the assassination was "clearly related to the genocide," as it was the "trigger that started the genocide."

Suppressing evidence of the assassination's perpetrator has been crucial in the West, as it seems awkward that the "trigger" for "The Genocide" was ultimately pulled, not by the officially designated Hutu villains, but by the Tutsi victors in this conflict, the RPF, long-supported by the United States and by its close allies (who very possibly aided the assassins in the shoot-down). It has also been important to suppress the fact that the first Hutu president of Burundi, Melchior Ndadaye, had been assassinated by Tutsi officers in his army in October 1993, an action celebrated by the RPF and arousing fears among Rwanda's Hutu.

A far more comprehensive eight-year investigation by the French magistrate Jean-Louis Bruguière, who had been asked to rule on the deaths of the three French nationals operating the government jet that was shot down in April 1994, concluded that the assassination followed from Kagame's rejection of the Arusha power-sharing accords of August 1993, and that for Kagame, the "physical elimination" of Habyarimana was therefore essential to achieving the goal of an RPF-takeover in Rwanda. Bruguière issued nine arrest warrants for high-ranking RPF members close to Kagame, and requested that the ICTR itself take up Kagame's prosecution, as under French law, Bruguière could not issue an arrest warrant for a head of state.

Rwanda Experienced a Genocide

Gerald Caplan

In the following viewpoint, the author argues that Edward S. Herman and David Peterson—the authors of the previous viewpoint—are wrong in their contention that there was no genocide of the Hutus in Rwanda. He maintains that Herman and Peterson's account contradicts the scholarly consensus, is poorly sourced, and is disproved by a mass of first-person testimony. He says that Herman and Peterson are leftist anti-imperialists who have convinced themselves that the United States is the source of all evil in the world, and that the United States backed the Tutsis in Rwanda. The author concludes that the United States did in fact act poorly in Rwanda by failing to intervene and is responsible for many atrocities in many parts of the world. However, he writes, denying the Rwandan genocide in order to attack the United States is foolish and immoral. Gerald Caplan is a Canadian researcher, writer, and political activist specializing in African history and the author of Rwanda: The Preventable Genocide *and* The Betrayal of Africa.

This is a review of Edward S. Herman and David Peterson's *The Politics of Genocide*, Monthly Review Press, New York, 2010.

Edward Herman is a professor emeritus at the University of Pennsylvania and David Peterson is described as a Chicago-based journalist and researcher. Those who have read Herman's work, some of it in collaboration with Noam Chomsky, will only partly know what to expect from his latest book. Herman and Peterson argue that in a world controlled by the American empire and its media and intellectual lackeys, genocide has become a political construct largely manipulated by Washington and its allies. The claim of genocide becomes an excuse for so-called humanitarian intervention that disguises malevolent imperial motives: 'The Western establishment rushed to proclaim "genocide" in Bosnia-Herzegovina, Rwanda, Kosovo, and Darfur. . . . In contrast, its silence over the crimes committed by its own regimes against the peoples of Southeast Asia, Central America, the Middle East and sub-Saharan Africa is deafening. This is the "politics of genocide".'

Herman and Peterson give some examples that should be familiar to all who reject the notion of the US as an unparalleled force for good in the world. The suffering of Iraqis under US-led sanctions in the 1990s, American support for Israel's repression in Gaza and destruction in Lebanon, the American role in the brutal massacres of Guatemalans and Salvadorans in the 1980s, America's backing for Indonesia's blood bath in East Timor—all are true, all are appalling, and all have been thoroughly documented. No doubt it's good for a new generation to be reminded of these atrocities, invariably distorted or ignored by the mainstream media. But I'm not at all sure that it's helpful to explore these issues against a frame of genocide, and it's supremely destructive that incontrovertible incidents of American crimes, such as the above, are included with bizarre fictions that have poisoned the authors' minds, such as below. This was decidedly unexpected from Edward Herman.

Deniers Have Their Own Agenda

To this stage, this little volume might on balance just be considered recommended reading. Despite its strange biases and excesses in belabouring its thesis, it's a useful reminder of American double standards that should not be forgotten (particularly given the disappointing record of the [US president Barack] Obama administration).

But all of this is mere preliminary for Herman and Peterson. Their main target, which is none of the cases mentioned so far, can be found squarely in the heart of the book. It's chapter 4, the longest single section, and its purpose is to show that the 1994 genocide of the Rwandan Tutsi never happened. In fact the entire 'genocide' in Rwanda is an elaborate American conspiracy to 'gain a strong military presence in Central Africa, a diminution of its European rivals' influence, proxy armies to serve its interests, and access to the raw material–rich Democratic Republic of the Congo'. The authors' greatest bete noir is Paul Kagame, commander of the Rwandan Patriotic Front (RPF) rebels during the 1990–94 civil war and 1994 genocide, long-time president of post-genocide Rwanda—and leading Yankee stooge.

Yes, in order to blame the American empire for every ill on earth, Herman and Peterson, two dedicated anti-imperialists, have sunk to the level of genocide deniers. And the 'evidence' they adduce to back up their delusional tale rests solidly on a foundation of other deniers, statements by genocidaires, fabrications, distortions, innuendo and gross ignorance. In this Grimm fairy tale, everyone who contradicts their fantasies is an American/RPF pawn—Paul Kagame, human rights investigator Alison des Forges, the head of the UN military mission in Rwanda during the genocide General Romeo Dallaire, and entire human rights organisations. . . .

Deniers Are Selective with Their Sources

As for Alison Des Forges, until her untimely death perhaps the most prominent scholar and activist on the Rwanda file, she is

dismissed as following: '[Prior to 1993], des Forges had worked
for the US Department of State and National Security Council.'
Nothing more is said to disqualify des Forges, so we must conclude that simply working for these bodies demonstrates the un-
reliability of her views on the genocide. That her MA and Ph.D.
theses were on Rwandan history, that she knew the country for
30 years before the genocide, that she was among a tiny number of outsiders who spoke Kinyarwanda, that she spent five
years after 1994 researching the crisis, that her *Leave None to
Tell the Story* is a highly-respected encyclopaedic history of the
genocide—all this is irrelevant to Herman and Peterson. In their
obsessive anti-Americanism, they blithely smear des Forges's entire life: 'Alison Des Forges's career is best understood in terms
of the services she performed on behalf of US power-projection
in Central Africa, with this policy-oriented work couched in the
rhetoric of 'human rights'. In the process, Des Forges badly mis-
informed a whole generation of scholars, activists, and the cause
of peace and justice.' But if she was such a loyal American hack,
why was she such an unrestrained critic of America's great ally
Kagame? This obvious contradiction is of no apparent interest to
Herman and Peterson.

The work of the 1993 International Commission of Inquiry
into Human Rights Abuses in Rwanda is similarly dismissed.
The Inquiry brought together four well-known human rights organisations whose investigation led them to conclude that the
Habyarimana government was deliberately targeting Tutsi for
massacre, that extremists' anti-Tutsi rhetoric was growing and
that anti-Tutsi militia were being formed. Yet none of this needs
to be taken seriously. Why? Because the Commission was little
more than an RPF front, 'either directly funded by the RPF or in-
filtrated by it'. The sole source for this very serious accusation—
made by no others of whom I'm aware—is Robin Philpot, Canada's preeminent denier of the genocide.

Is Philpot's charge remotely credible? Has he exposed some
deep conspiracy no one else has ever detected? By coincidence, I

know both the person who initiated the Commission of Inquiry, Ed Broadbent, and one of its members, William Schabas. (Alison Des Forges was another member, representing Human Rights Watch.) Instead of just dismissing the Philpot charge, I asked each of them about the Commission. Broadbent, a former leader of the New Democratic Party of Canada, was then the president of Rights and Democracy, an independent Canadian-based international human rights organisation funded by the Conservative government of the day. I spoke to him by phone. Rumours of foul doings in Rwanda took him to the country in 1992, he told me, and he was so shaken by the evidence he found of violence and discrimination against the Tutsi minority that he organised and mostly funded the International Commission to follow up his work. He told me he is simply incredulous that anyone would claim a role for the RPF in its work, since it wasn't true.

Broadbent asked William Schabas, then professor of human rights law at the Université du Québec à Montréal, to represent Rights and Democracy in this investigation. Schabas is now director of the Irish Centre for Human Rights at the National University of Ireland in Galway, where he also holds the chair in human rights law. In an email, Schabas told me he had never been to Rwanda before this mission and knew nothing about the country. 'I certainly never detected any pro-RPF sentiment from Ed. . . . There was one member who seemed to be a sympathiser of the RPF. . . . Otherwise, many members were quite openly critical of or hostile to the RPF.'

Is this just a case of 'he said–they said'? Does an open-minded reader consider that the accusations of Robin Philpot, a man who also believes General Dallaire was an American stooge, are as worthy of consideration as the two statements by Ed Broadbent and William Schabas? Are both Broadbent and Schabas, 17 years later, blatantly lying to me, just as Dallaire's entire life for the past 17 years must be a lie?

Or does one rather draw another conclusion about how the deniers operate? If there are views that contradict your own, you simply dismiss them as tools of either the US State Department or the RPF. Further proof is not required.

Evidence of American Manipulation Is Weak

Let me cite the authors themselves to assure readers I haven't exaggerated or distorted their extraordinary re-writing of history. Chapter 4 of their little book is devoted to Rwanda and the Congo and its 18 pages constitute far and away their longest case study.

They begin by asserting that 'the Western establishment [has] swallowed a propaganda line on Rwanda that turned perpetrator and victim upside-down'. In their Rwanda story, it's not Hutu extremists, the Presidential Guard, the post-Habyarimana interim government and the interahamwe militia who were the 'prime genocidaires'. It was the RPF. As a matter of fact, 'the Hutu members of Rwanda's power-sharing government couldn't possibly have planned a genocide against the Tutsi'. In fact, President Habyarimana repeatedly refused, until literally the end of his life, to implement the power-sharing agreement set out in the Arusha Accords. In any event, why the Hutu members of the government 'couldn't possibly have planned a genocide against the Tutsi' is never remotely explained.

Next: The 1990 invasion of Rwanda from Uganda was carried out not by Rwandans but by Ugandan forces under Ugandan President Museveni, the RPF being 'a wing of the Ugandan army'. There is no source given for this assertion, which contradicts almost all other histories of the invasion.

'It is clear that Museveni and the RPF were perceived as serving US interests and that the government of President Habyarimana was targeted for ouster. . . . The Ugandan army and the RPF were doing what the United States wanted done in Rwanda.' This is the central thesis of the entire chapter on Rwanda, but the only source who actually 'perceives' matters this way seems to be Robin Philpot, the Canadian who denies the genocide, since he is the only source offered for this categorical assertion. No other historian of the genocide of whom I'm aware makes this claim and no evidence for it exists.

Turning Linda Melvern's seminal book 'Conspiracy to Murder' on its head, the authors give us 'an RPF conspiracy' to overthrow the Hutu government and capture the state for themselves. Since one of their sources, Christopher Black, considers Melvern part of the 'RPF–US propaganda machine', she too can be dismissed. But then why, they want to know, has the International Criminal Tribunal for Rwanda (ICTR) 'never once entertained the question of this conspiracy?' This is indeed a reasonable question; I wondered about it myself. Here is their answer: 'This, we believe, flows from US and allied support of the RPF, reflected in media coverage, humanitarian intellectuals' and NGO activism, as well as the ICTR's jurisprudence.' In other words, a giant US-led conspiracy is at work here.

Dupes like me and most other writers believe the US and its allies betrayed Rwanda by refusing to reinforce the UN military mission there, as general Dallaire was pleading with them to do. Eyewitnesses in Rwanda believed they witnessed for themselves what was developing. The media actually played a deplorable role in the first month of the genocide, confusing a planned extermination with racist views of 'primordial African savagery'. And the many different ICTR judges over 15 years, from around the globe, all pretended to base their findings on the legal evidence. Yet in reality, all this time everyone was subtly being manipulated by the United States. Indeed, so subtle was the manipulation that the devilishly cunning Yanks left no proof of it. Moreover, every leading member of the [Bill] Clinton administration, including the president himself, [first lady] Hillary Clinton and Madeleine Albright, after her stint as ambassador to the UN as Clinton's Secretary of State, have shamefacedly admitted abandoning the Tutsi. Each claims to consider it perhaps the greatest regret of his/her time in office, merely demonstrating, of course, what unconscionable hypocrites they are. . . .

Deniers Recast Hutu Genocidaires as Dead Hutu Victims

Herman and Peterson now take their argument further. They have concluded that the all-important conventionally-accepted truth about the 100 days of genocide is all wrong. In fact this was no genocide at all against the Tutsi in which at a minimum 500,000/600,000 and perhaps as many as a million unarmed Tutsi were slaughtered, along with many Hutu who wouldn't co-operate with the extremists' genocidal conspiracy. On the contrary. They cite the sensational estimate by Christian Davenport and Allan Stam that one million deaths occurred from April to July 1994, and that 'the majority of victims are likely Hutu and not Tutsi.' That the methodology employed to arrive at such an Orwellian assertion has been totally discredited is of no interest to our authors and never mentioned.

Indeed, even a million dead, mostly Hutu, isn't good enough for them. They refer to 'a number of observers as well as participants in the events of 1994 [who] claim that the great majority of deaths were Hutu, with some estimates as high as two million.' With Herman and Peterson, you always have to watch your wallets. Checking the endnote for this rather extravagant statement, we find the figure comes from 'a former RPF military officer Christophe Hakizimana' in a letter to the 1999 UN Commission of Inquiry into the genocide. But that Commission, chaired by former Swedish Prime Minister Ingvar Carlsson, hadn't the slightest doubt that genocide against the Tutsi had taken place and their report harshly criticised the US and its allies for refusing to intervene to stop it. So it's hardly surprising that the Inquiry's report never mentions Hakizimana and his accusations.

So how did our authors know about it? 'We base this on personal communications with the international criminal lawyer Christopher Black of Toronto.' It will by this time come as no surprise to readers to learn that Christopher Black is prominent among the small notorious band of deniers who cite each other so faithfully and who alone are the sources for Herman and

Peterson's chapter 4. Even among the lunatic fringe of deniers, Black inhabits a universe of his own. Not only is the genocide of the Tutsi a 'myth', not only did France have nothing to do with it, not only did the RPF rampage 'across the country massacring hundreds of thousands of Hutu and any Tutsi who were seen as non-reliable.' As well, he asserts, before 1994 there was no ethnic problem in Rwanda, then 'a semi-socialist country considered a model for Africa'. For perspective, I note that this authority on Rwanda visited North Korea in 2003 and emerged to describe it as 'a progressive, socialist country deserving the support of all progressive peoples around the world.' Black also considered [Yugoslav president] Slobodan Milosevic completely innocent of the charges brought against him and believes Milosevic was consistently committed to a multi-ethnic Yugoslavia during his time in government.

Yet [Christophe Hakizimana and Christopher Black] are the two sources Herman and Peterson give for their stunning statement that 'a number of observers as well as participants in the events of 1994 claim that the great majority of deaths were Hutu, with some estimates as high as two million.'

The authors simply dismiss out of hand the widely-accepted facts about the genocide. 'The established narrative's 800,000 or more largely Tutsi deaths resulting from a "preprogrammed genocide" committed by "Hutu Power" appears to have no basis in any facts beyond the early claims by Kagame's RPF and its politically motivated Western sponsors and propagandists.' With this single sentence, and with no further amplification of any kind, the question of the number of Tutsi murdered is closed.

But there's much more about murdered Hutu. It is no surprise to the authors that the RPF killed so many people. After all, 'the RPF was the only well-organised killing force within Rwanda in 1994. . . . Clearly the chief responsibility for Rwanda political violence belongs to the RPF, and not to the ousted coalition government, the FAR [Rwandan army], or any Hutu-related group.' So much for the interahamwe, apparently figments of everyone's imagination. And for the Hutu Power and Zero Network hit lists, which many diplomats actually saw. And for the explicit public threats against the Tutsi from RTLM [Radio Télévision Libre des Mille Collines] hate radio and *Kangura* magazine. In the report I wrote for the International Panel of Eminent Persons appointed by the Organization of African Unity to investigate the genocide, there is a chapter titled 'The Eve of the Genocide: What the World Knew'. The report, published in 2000 and called *Rwanda: The Preventable Genocide*, is still available online, so readers can access it in full, as indeed could Herman and Peterson. . . .

American Anti-Imperialists Have Gone Too Far

Edward Herman and David Peterson have written a very short book that's not nearly short enough. It should never have seen the light of day. It brings shame to its two American authors, its publisher Monthly Review, and all those who have provided enthusiastic jacket blurbs, many of them prominent in progressive circles—Noam Chomsky, John Pilger, Norman Solomon, David Barsamian. If this is what Anglo-American Marxism, or socialism, or anti-imperialism has degenerated into, we can hang our heads in shame for the future of the left.

Why a lifetime anti-imperialist leftist like Herman (and presumably Peterson) wants to exculpate the Serbs of Bosnia, Croatia and Serbia of crimes against humanity is beyond my understanding. Why would it not have been enough to point out that appalling crimes were committed by all sides, but in every case Serbs were one of those sides? The only conceivable reason seems to be that the US and its allies singled out the Serbs for attack, which ipso facto makes them the real victims. Indeed, the authors' ally Christopher Black perversely sees Milosevic as an heroic figure.

As we've already seen, hyperbole and slipperiness are cherished tools of the authors, and not just in regards to Rwanda. 'The leading mainstream experts on "genocide" and mass-atrocity crimes today,' they assert, 'still carefully exclude from consideration the US attacks on Indo-China as well as the 1965–1966 Indonesian massacres within that country'. First note the way they add 'mass atrocity crimes' to genocidal crimes. In fact, in many circles it surely remains widely accepted that the US was guilty of appalling atrocities in its aggressions against Viet Nam, Laos and Cambodia. As for the 'exclusion from consideration' of those Indonesian massacres, chapter 7 of Totten and Parson's popular volume 'Century of Genocide', is titled 'The Indonesian Massacres'.

Two other similar examples: In true conspiratorial fashion, they argue that the crisis in Darfur was exaggerated to distract attention from America's real African interest, the mineral resources of the Congo. Why both weren't worthy of serious attention is beyond me. Nonetheless, they insist that Darfur solidarity activists dishonestly succeeded in framing Darfur as the 'unnoticed genocide', though many, including me, have long understood that it's been the best publicised international crisis in decades. And they charge that it's the calamity in eastern Congo that 'has been truly ignored', even though numerous celebrities, including playwright Eve Ensler (*The Vagina Monologues*), actor Ben Affleck (at least four times), UN Secretary-General Ban Ki-moon and Secretary of State Hillary Clinton have all made high-profile visits to the Kivus [region in the Democratic Republic of Congo]. When the US Secretary of State visits a small province in eastern Congo, you know it's the opposite of being ignored.

Many of the Rwanda deniers flaunt their left-wing credentials. As this essay makes clear, they are driven by their anti-Americanism. Certainly I agree that every progressive necessarily must be anti-American to some degree or other. But this little band has driven over the edge. As Peter Erlinder once wrote, America is 'the most dangerous Empire the world has ever seen'. Everything bad must be America's responsibility. There's not even room for others to share that responsibility, though the French government's complicity in the Rwandan genocide, for example, has been definitively documented and is now [June 2010] even implicitly accepted by [French] President Sarkozy and his foreign minister Bernard Kouchner.

Why the deniers are so determined, so passionate, so intransigent, so absolutely certain, so satisfied to remain part of a tiny minority of cranks, is completely unknown to me. Why they want to create such gratuitous, almost sadistic hurt for the survivors of the genocide in Rwanda is impossible to fathom. But in the end, it's irrelevant what furies drive their obsessions. It's their egregious views—not their motives—that matter. And their views relegate them squarely to the lunatic fringe.

Rwanda: Fifty Years of Ethnic Conflict on Steroids

Herman J. Cohen

The author of the following viewpoint maintains that ethnic tensions between Hutus and Tutsis were exacerbated by colonial rule. Subsequently, the author writes, the conflict between Tutsis and Hutus resulted in three genocides: the first by Tutsis against Hutus in Burundi 1972; the second was the well-known Hutu genocide of Tutsis in Rwanda in 1994; and finally a Tutsi attack on Hutu refugees in the eastern region of the Democratic Republic of the Congo (DRC). The author writes that the situation in the eastern DRC is still unstable, and that ethnic tensions remain a serious problem in Rwanda. He concludes that another genocide in the region is possible. Herman J. Cohen served in the US Foreign Service until 1993, when he founded the consulting firm Cohen and Woods International.

The 1994 genocide in the central African Republic of Rwanda was the inevitable result of a long history of ethnic tension in an overpopulated, impoverished nation. The colonial experience under European rule destabilized what was a historic symbiotic relationship between the majority Hutu and minority

Herman J. Cohen, "Rwanda: Fifty Years of Ethnic Conflict on Steroids," *Journal of the National Committee on American Foreign Policy*, vol. 34, no. 2, April 26, 2012, pp. 86–92.

Tutsi ethnic populations. The challenges of independence and self-government deepened ethnic polarization, creating refugees in neighboring countries and repression internally. The civil war of 1990–1994 resulted in the genocidal murders of 800,000 innocent civilians. When it ended, the minority Tutsis were in power. But there were repercussions in the neighboring eastern Congo where perpetrators of genocide took refuge. An eight-year war in the eastern Congo, resulting from the spill-over of ethnic tensions in Rwanda, witnessed yet another genocide and the needless deaths of more than five million Congolese from disease, malnutrition, and mass violence. The international community did not distinguish itself in dealing with either the Rwandan genocide of 1994 or the ensuing violence in the eastern Congo. A repetition of these experiences cannot be ruled out because ethnic tensions in Rwanda continue to simmer, and armed militias continue to pillage, rape, and kill in the eastern Congo. The United Nations declaration on the "Responsibility to Protect" resulted from the Rwanda debacle and is slowly gaining acceptability.

Normally, readers of international news would not expect to see much press coverage of the tiny Republic of Rwanda, an independent country the size of the state of Maryland, sitting in the "Great Lakes" region of east-central Africa. But ever since 1994, when a horrific event occurred in Rwanda, this country continues to receive significant world attention. That event, of course, was the genocide perpetrated on the minority Tutsi ethnic group, resulting in the deliberate murder of approximately 800,000 men, women, and children. The conclusion that these killings came under the internationally recognized definition of genocide was certified by the U.S. State Department during the administration of President George W. Bush.[1]

The Rwandan genocide of 1994 was not a singular event. It was the super-climax of an ethnic conflict that began in 1959, reached a crescendo in 1994, and continues today. It should be studied to examine the relationship between ethnicity and civil conflict, both violent and nonviolent. A study of the reaction of the international community to the Rwandan genocide, both during and afterward, can also be quite an eye-opener to foreign affairs practitioners. The relatively new United Nations concept known as "responsibility to protect" was crafted largely in response to the Rwandan genocide. How, in the future, will the international community move to protect innocent civilians being massacred within sovereign borders?[2]

How the Colonials Intensified Ethnic Differences

European powers colonized Africa during the nineteenth century, with final boundaries being drawn from Europe's African colonies at the Berlin Conference of 1885. From this point, the Europeans administered their respective colonies pursuant to their own sociopolitical norms. Unfortunately, Rwanda, and its ethnically similar neighbor Burundi, were governed first by pre–World War I Germany and second by the Kingdom of Belgium. Neither of these powers, in their day, could be called benevolent or intelligent.

Both Rwanda and Burundi enjoy rich volcanic soils and lie close to the equator on relatively low hills along high plateaus that provide excellent conditions for growing coffee, tea, and other tropical foodstuffs. Accordingly, a variety of peoples migrated to these very attractive territories. From the eleventh century, Bantu linguistic groups moved into Rwanda from points west, mainly from the country now known as the Democratic Republic of the Congo. These groups were farmers. At the same time, Nilotic linguistic groups moved south from sections (believed to be in present-day Ethiopia) of the Nile basin's great rift. These groups were pastoral, with significant livestock herds that served as family wealth.

The farmers came to be known as "Hutu"; the pastoralists called themselves "Tutsi." Over the centuries, through intermarriage and crowded living conditions, the two ethnic groups developed a single common Bantu language—Kinyarwanda—as well as a monarchial government system headed by a royal individual knows as "the Mwami," or king. The Mwamis always came from the pastoral community, but both Tutsis and Hutus served as royal courtiers and lived harmoniously. The vast majority of both communities have always lived in rural areas and have been dirt poor. Only a small class of privileged civil service and business individuals and families enjoyed the luxury of urban living and life somewhat above the poverty line. In terms of numbers, the pastoralist Tutsi make up 15 percent and the Hutus 75 percent of the population.[3]

The arrival of the colonial powers in the nineteenth and early twentieth centuries, first the Germans and then the Belgians, resulted in the clear sociopolitical determination that the minority Tutsis had a more "advanced intelligence." Hence, the colonial powers engaged in the self-fulfilling prophecy of privileging the Tutsis for education, jobs in the civil service, and business licensing. A deep ethnic divide was thus created. Tutsis were on top, while the majority Hutu community was on the bottom.[4]

Colonialism Winds Down and Ethnic Conflict Erupts

During the early 1950s, agitation within Africa, and pressure from pro-self-determination powers, especially the United States, caused the European colonialists to start preparations for transitions to independence throughout their colonial empires. The driving concept was to advance the colonies toward multiparty democratic systems similar to their own. With their well-developed colonial administrations, the French and the British were able to move systematically to prepare future leaders and help build basic institutions as absolute prerequisites to post-independence stability.[5]

Belgium, on the other hand, had little interest in the idea of self-determination for its African colonies, especially the giant Congo to the immediate west of the tiny Rwanda and Burundi colonies. In addition, because of its own ethnic and political tensions, Belgium experienced internal conflict over the entire independence process. Belgian socialist colonial administrators engineered an overthrow of the Tutsi Mwami in Rwanda in the year 1959. This Hutu "revolution" let to revenge-style pogroms against the Tutsi community, resulting in 160,000 of the latter fleeing to neighboring countries as refugees. In Burundi, on the other hand, Belgian conservative colonials made sure that the newly independent government remained firmly in the hands of Tutsi elites, protected by Tutsi military officers. The bottom line for both Rwanda and Burundi was that independence uncovered a seething undercurrent of ethnic tensions—ready to explode as soon as the Belgian protective cover was lifted.

Persecution of Tutsis continued in Rwanda after formal independence in 1962, thereby swelling the ranks of refugees in neighboring countries, especially in Uganda to the immediate north. Within ten years, both Rwanda and Burundi were controlled by military leaders who had carried out coups d'état. In 1970, the Rwandan government declared that Tutsis living in exile would never be allowed to return because of the lack of space, thereby contravening international conventions. Needless to say, the Tutsi communities living in exile reached the conclusion that the only way to return would be to force their way back, thereby giving rise to serious military plotting. This was reinforced by the feeling among the largest Tutsi refugee group, those in Uganda, that true integration into Ugandan society would never be feasible.[6]

The Saga of Three Great Lakes Genocides

Burundi 1972

Burundi, in 1972, was the birthplace of the idea of genocide as a solution to ethnic tensions and the struggle for power in central Africa. By that year, the number of Hutus educated beyond the fifth grade had become substantial. With encouragement from the outside, especially the exile community in Europe, the educated Hutus began agitating for majority rule. After all, they argued, minority rule by a small African ethnic minority in Burundi was just as bad as minority rule by a small white population in South Africa.

The Tutsi minority regime ruling Burundi was not complacent in the face of the agitation for majority rule by educated Hutu. As the Tutsi saw themselves as essentially "condemned" to rule (or die), they also saw only one way to stay in power—that way was to arrange for the murder of every Hutu with a fifth grade or higher education. Before neighboring Tanzania was able to exert crucial pressure on their transportation system, the Burundi Tutsi elites managed to murder approximately 80,000 Hutu citizens. For accounting purposes, we might designate the Burundi ethnic massacres of 1972 as the "First Great Lakes Genocide." The perpetrators of the Burundi genocide were in no way called to account, thus allowing the idea that this method of resolving ethnic conflicts in the sub-region was acceptable and even quasi-normal.

In the United States in the early 1970s, human rights were not a high priority on the foreign affairs agenda. In this sector, the major focus was on civil rights for African Americans and other minorities internal to the United States. But the Burundi massacres caught the attention of some Democratic members of Congress who wanted to know why the Nixon administration had stood idly by. Hearings were held that had administration witnesses claiming that everything possible had been done diplomatically. Indeed, State Department pressure on the president of Tanzania—threats to stop rail traffic to Burundi—was responsible for the decision to end the killings. Much skepticism was expressed about Nixon's policy toward foreign massacres by the foreign affairs committees. The net result, however, was that human rights would eventually become a major element in U.S. foreign policy worldwide, not just within the Soviet orbit. Within a few years of the Burundi genocide, Congress instituted the annual "Human Rights Report" covering all foreign countries receiving American assistance. Human rights issues could no longer be ignored at high foreign policy levels.

Rwanda 1994

Rwandan Tutsis living in exile as a result of the government-sponsored pogroms between 1959 and 1962 were concentrated in Uganda, Burundi, and the Democratic Republic of the Congo. The population living in Uganda, mostly within fifty miles of the Rwandan border, was by far the most numerous. Within this population, the political passions for a return to Rwanda, by arms if necessary, were the most intense.

The Rwandan Tutsis who were small children during the 1959–1962 exodus, or who were born in Ugandan refugee villages, were adults in their 30s and 40s by the year 1990 when all hell broke loose on the Ugandan-Rwandan border. The Ugandan military had a number of Rwandan Tutsis who were making their careers as officers in a variety of specialties, including intelligence. These ethnic Tutsis chose to support Ugandan president Yoweri Museveni when he led rebel forces to overthrow the corrupt authoritarian dictatorships of Idi Amin and Milton Obote between 1979 and 1986. As a result of their support of the winner, the Tutsi officers prospered in their Ugandan military careers, with several reaching senior ranks.[7]

From 1986, when Ugandan President Museveni consolidated his power, to 1990, when war broke out on the Uganda-Rwandan border, the Rwandan Tutsis in the Ugandan army spent a lot of time plotting the armed return of their community to their Rwandan homeland. This was especially true of a cell within the intelligence division. This group was in a particular hurry because the Hutu military dictatorship in Rwanda was beginning to soften under international donor pressure. President Juvenal Habyarimana started to talk about instituting multiparty democracy in 1988, actually authorizing the formation of political parties in 1989–1990. As a result, several parties were formed that were a mixture of Hutu and Tutsi intellectuals. Thus, ethnic barriers were being broken down among the educated class.[8]

Of even greater concern to the Tutsi military plotters in the Ugandan army was Habyarimana's softening on the issue of the right of return of the refugees. He had steadfastly held to the decision that the Tutsis would not be allowed to return to Rwanda because there was no room in that small, densely populated country. He even reiterated that policy in a public pronouncement in 1990. But, behind the scenes, Habyarimana indicated a willingness to consider a controlled return.[9]

Needless to say, the Tutsi officers in Uganda did not want a change of Rwandan policy with respect to the return of refugees. The right of return of refugees was important, but even more important was the reestablishment of Tutsi minority rule. This could only be achieved through conquest. Hence, accelerating the pace of plotting for an invasion was necessary.

On October 1, 1990, the Rwandan Tutsi insurgency against the government of Juvenal Habyarimana began with three hundred armed guerrillas crossing the border from Uganda. The insurgents were all soldiers in the Ugandan army. This initial operation grew into a full-scale civil war, with the Rwandan government enlarging its army fivefold, and the international

Members of the Rwandan Patriotic Army (RPA) prepare for their march on Rwanda's capital city, Kigali, on May 25, 1994. The RPA included Rwandan Tutsi soldiers who had been exiled in Uganda. © Scott Peterson/Liaison/Getty Images.

community making every effort to engage in conflict resolution. From 1990 to 1994, there were cease-fires, negotiations under the auspices of the Intergovernmental Association for African Development (IGAAD), an East African economic community, a peace treaty with power-sharing signed in Arusha, Tanzania, in 1993, and much churning within the politics of each side. None of these efforts brought real peace to Rwanda because neither side really wanted peace short of its own outright victory.[10]

After a long cease-fire, large-scale fighting broke out again on April 6, 1994, triggered by the shooting down of an executive aircraft returning President Habyarimana from a meeting in Tanzania. The president's death began a three-month period of mass killing of Tutsis, as well as Hutus who had worked with Tutsis in the new political parties. The regime had decided that the only way to defeat the insurgents was to kill all the Tutsis, thereby leaving the Tutsi insurgents without a population to swim in. the way it was carried out gave evidence of careful preparation for the genocide.

The Tutsi insurgents decided that their first priority was to defeat the Rwandan army, gain power, and finally stop any further killing. The insurgents were under orders to avoid becoming involved in countering any genocidal killings they came across as they advanced. They were operating under the name "Rwanda Patriotic Army" (RPA). Unfortunately, a full three months were needed for the three thousand RPA fighters to accomplish their military objective of taking power in Kigali, the capital, and driving out the official Rwandan army. In those three months, as many as 800,000 civilians, mostly Tutsi, were massacred because of their ethnicity. It was a cut-and-dried case of premeditated genocide. In addition to the mass killings, one million people fled Rwanda and another million were displaced.

Unlike the 1972 genocide against Hutus in Burundi, the 1994 genocide in Rwanda against Tutsis caused quite a stir in international circles. Accompanied by much finger pointing, the question of why no nation moved to intervene to save lives—except for a last-minute French military mission, under UN mandate, that actually did save as many as 50,000 Tutsis—was raised.[11] The UN investigations, the congressional hearings, and lots of academic research brought forth a lot of breast-beating and multitudinous promises of "never again." One significant result was the establishment of a special international criminal tribunal to indict and try perpetrators of the Rwandan genocide. After the disaster that had befallen American special forces in Somalia a year earlier, the U.S. government was not about to intervene in Rwanda nor allow the UN to intervene.[12]

Presumably, the RPA victory in Rwanda, the consolidation of power by the victors, and the return of more than half a million exiled Tutsis and their livestock from Uganda, Burundi, and the Congo, were supposed to bring peace at last to Rwanda. Alas, this was not to be the case.

The Eastern Congo 1996

As the RPA approached their final objective, the capital city of Kigali, up to one million Hutus, along with government military personnel, political murderers, and assorted leadership, fled to neighboring Congo where they set up refugee camps close to the border. The UN High Commission for Refugees (UNHCR) became involved in the care and feeding of these exiles.

One major difference in this refugee situation was that the camps became a Rwandan government in exile, with a full disciplinary organization. In effect, the military dictatorship and a significant part of the population moved across the border. The objective, of course, was to fight their way back into Rwanda and reclaim power. To that end they began trafficking in arms and selling humanitarian relief goods to earn money. The exiles were supported by the Congolese military who were happy to sell arms. These former Rwandan army personnel and militias were carrying out cross-border raids against the Rwandan regime. The UNHCR turned a blind eye to all of this; the new government in Rwanda, on the other hand considered these armed groups on its border to be a major threat and continued to demand that the international community respond. The implied threat: if the international community could not resolve the issue, then the Rwandan government would take direct action.

This very unstable situation on the Congo-Rwanda border continued for two years. In md-1996, the Rwandan government started receiving unsubtle hints from international sources that taking action against the refugee camps would not be criticized.[13]

In October 1996, the Rwandan army made its move to break up the refugee camps. However, the action was more than just a quick strike to eliminate an irritation. Rather, it was a well-planned action to overthrow the Mobutu government in the Congo, utilizing a surrogate Congolese guerrilla force known as the Alliance of Democratic Forces for the Liberation of the Congo (AFDL) under Laurent Kabila, a longtime Congolese exile.[14]

The Rwandan army onslaught very quickly destroyed and emptied the camps, with about 800,000 Hutu refugees moving back into Rwanda and about 200,000 fleeing westward deeper into the Congo (along with all the former military and other assorted perpetrators of the genocide). Instead of returning to Rwanda, the new Rwandan government forces then moved westward into the Congo in two thrusts. The first moved Laurent Kabila and his Congolese insurgents toward the capital city of Kinshasa to overthrow the 31-year Mobutu dictatorship. The second was in pursuit of the 200,000 Hutu refugees who had decided not to return home but to continue to move farther away from Rwanda with their ex-military escorts.

The first thrust toward Kinshasa succeeded within two months, with the help of the army of Angola that had nothing but animosity toward Mobutu who continued to give safe haven to insurgents in that country. The ousted Mobutu went into exile, while Laurent Kabila, with his Rwandan handlers, took power in Kinshasa.

As for the second thrust in pursuit of Hutus who refused to return to Rwanda, the Rwandan Patriotic Army caught up with them near the major city of Kisangani, where the mighty Congo River begins its one thousand mile flow to the ocean. There, in a village area known as Tingi Tingi, the Rwandan military, with their Congolese surrogates, methodically separated Rwandan citizens from Congolese villagers who welcomed them. The Rwandans—men, women, and children—were murdered. The total killed was estimated to be about 80,000 Hutus. This was the third Great Lakes genocide—this time against Hutus. Ironically, the original perpetrators of the Rwandan genocide escaped to neighboring countries, including the Central African Republic and the Democratic Republic of the Congo. They returned to fighting in 1996 when war broke out between Rwanda and the Congo. The paranoid new Rwandan regime viewed all Hutus who continued their westward march, refusing to return to Rwanda, as de facto genocide supporters. Hence, they had to be eliminated.

The Tingi Tingi massacres were common knowledge in the Congo because the surviving villagers did not hesitate to speak of them and the knowledge was transmitted widely. The government of Rwanda denied the allegations, but a long and meticulous investigation by UN personnel proved that the Rwandan army did, indeed perpetrate this genocide against a Hutu refugee population in the eastern Congo.[15]

War between the Congo and Rwanda broke out in August 1996 with President Kabila having fallen out with his original mentors in the Rwandan government. Since then, the eastern Congo has remained a very unstable region, with millions of unnecessary deaths from starvation, disease, and war. As analysts describe the situation euphemistically, the eastern Democratic Republic of the Congo has suffered from the cross-border "fallout" of the Rwandan genocide and its aftermath.

Rwanda Faces the Future: Efficient Governance Within an Environment of Fear and Paranoia

Can we now say that the era of ethnic conflict in Rwanda is over? Can we truly say "never again" to genocide after the three perpetrated in 1971, 1994, and 1996? Unfortunately, Rwanda remains an unhappy country.

Ethnic minority rule is inherently unstable anywhere. In Rwanda, where the ruling elites represent only 15 percent of the population, the future looks ominous. Hutu intellectuals in Brussels, Paris, Nairobi, and South Africa continue to plot against the Rwandan regime and to finance anti-regime militias in the lawless eastern Congo. One of them, Victoria Ingabire returned to Rwanda from Europe in 2011 in order to participate in the presidential election. She was not allowed to run and was instead indicted for "genocide denial." Opposition politicians and critical journalists are being killed in fake automobile accidents; hit men are being sent to kill dissidents taking refuge in other African countries.

To make matters worse, the original "band of brothers" from the Tutsi group in the Ugandan army is beginning to splinter. Several of President Paul Kagame's top collaborators in the war to restore Tutsi hegemony have left Rwanda in fear of their lives or, in some cases, have been imprisoned. They, too, are engaged in plotting to effect regime change in Kagali.

There is some good news. President Paul Kagame has instituted governance that is developmental, efficient, corruption free, and designed to bring strong economic growth. But against a sociopolitical background of fear and paranoia, potential investors are unlikely to have sufficient confidence to bring projects and funds into the country.

Is another genocide possible in the Great Lakes sub-region? In view of the continuing ethnic tensions in Rwanda and neighboring Burundi, such a horrendous possibility cannot be discounted. Will the international community be in a position to fulfill the UN obligation to protect? So far, the track record has not been promising.

Notes

1. State Department declassified documents on the Rwanda Genocide, http://www.state.gov/m/a/ips/c44620.htm.

2. UN Secretary's address to the 2009 UN General Assembly special session on the responsibility to protect, www.un.org/News/Press/docs/2009/ga10845.doc.htm.
3. State Department, "Background Note" on Rwanda, November 30, 2011. Provides good short summary of Rwandan history, including interplay of the Hutu and Tutsi ethnic groups, http://www.state.gov/r/pa/ei/bgn/2861.htm.
4. *Ibid.*
5. Herman J. Cohen, "A Perspective of Fifty Years of U.S. Africa Policy: The Nixon Legacy," *American Foreign Policy Interests* 32, no. 4 (July/August 2010): 209–218.
6. The Hutu government in Rwanda had some logic on its side when it described the country as being too crowded to allow the Tutsi refugees to return, ever. Rwanda has the densest population in Africa at 435 persons per square kilometer. See CIA "World Factbook" chapter on Rwanda.
7. State Department: Country Reports: Uganda, October 21, 2011, www.state.gov/countryreports.
8. State Department: Country Reports: Rwanda, November 2011, www.state.gov/countryreports/Rwanda.
9. As Assistant Secretary of State for Africa, the author participated in several discussions with Rwandan government officials in 1989–1990, sponsored by the UN High Commission for Refugees, that considered the methodology for the return of refugees. The Tutsi officers in Uganda were aware of these discussions through their intelligence network.
10. Herman J. Cohen, "Intervening in Africa: Superpower Peace-making in a Troubled Continent," *Rwanda*, chapter 6 (New York: Macmillan/Palgrave, 2000), 163.
11. Wikipedia, "Operation Tourquoise," updated March 2011.
12. Established in 1994, the International Criminal Tribunal for Rwanda continued in operation as of early 2012, www.ictr.org.
13. Based on my conversations with U.S. diplomats during my travels in East Africa for the Global Coalition for Africa.
14. Department of State, Background Notes: Democratic Republic of the Congo, September 2011, http://www.state.gov/r/pa/ei/bgn/2823.htm.
15. "United Nations Mapping Report on Massacres in the Eastern Congo in 1994" (June 2010), http://www.rwandadocumentsproject.net.

The Rwandan Genocide Was a Political Conflict

Jane Hunter

In the following viewpoint, the author argues that most media have presented the conflicts in Rwanda as examples of African tribal ethnic tension. She asserts, however, that causes of violence in Rwanda are the result of a long political history of colonialism and inequity. France, in particular, has supported the Hutu government, helping to make the genocide possible and to protect the perpetrators, she explains. The view of the Rwandan genocide as an insoluble ethnic conflict is rooted in racism and colonialism, the author concludes. Jane Hunter is a writer for Extra!, *a publication of FAIR (Fairness and Accuracy in Reporting), a national media watchdog group.*

As a genocide it ranks with the century's biggest—the Armenians, the Jews, the Cambodians. But this spring, as Western officials marked the 50th anniversary of the Nazi Holocaust, no one—least of all the U.S. government—lifted a finger to stop the slaughter of hundreds of thousands of Rwandans. And U.S. media coverage played along with the [U.S. president Bill] Clinton administration's policy of handwringing.

France's Involvement in Rwanda

France, under [President] François Mitterrand, was the only Western nation to take an interest in Rwanda in the years leading up to, and including the period of the genocide. Unfortunately for its people, this interest was borne out in supporting a government that was intent on solving its political problems by mass murder. Paris had few qualms about its political and military backing for Habyarimana and the later interim government that organized and so effectively carried out the genocide. Each day, each cabinet meeting, each debriefing session of returning officials from Rwanda gave Mitterrand and his selected officials, who included his own son Jean-Christophe, the chance to admit a massive policy failure and to change tack. Instead, then, as now, the French government is in denial about the effects of its actions, and its responsibility second only to the murderers themselves, in the final genocide of the twentieth century. 'Never again' to Mitterrand spelled out only 'never without gain'; while there was perceived cultural and strategic value for France in keeping a genocidal government in place in Rwanda that took precedence over any amount of killing.

Andrew Wallis, "Preface," Silent Accomplice:
The Untold Story of France's Role in the
Rwandan Genocide. *New York: I.B. Tauris,*
2014, p. xi.

Almost daily since the Rwandan genocide began on April 6 [1994], broadcast media have aired horrific accounts and the major papers have featured the story on their front pages. The media seldom wavered, however, from their habitual racist portrayal of African strife as atavistic tribal savagery.

Occasionally, deep down in newspaper stories, the political context of the attacks on the Tutsi minority by members of the Hutu majority was acknowledged. But a reader seeking an explanation for Washington's inaction could read on through the end of May and come up empty. Instead of probing U.S. policy, the big media gave the Clinton administration an easy ride.

Hutu Political Hardliners Had French Support

Contrary to the media's endlessly reiterated theme, what is going on in Rwanda is not mindless tribal slaughter. The April 6 downing of an aircraft carrying Rwandan President Juvenal Habiyarimana and Burundian President Cyprien Ntaryamira—the incident that sparked the genocide—is widely believed to have been the work of Habiyarimana's own ruling clique, a hardline group bent on aborting a laboriously negotiated coalition government. That coalition would have brought the Tutsis into the Hutu-dominated government for the first time since Rwanda gained independence from Belgium in 1962; it would also have included democratic-minded Hutu opposition parties.

The hardliners, known as the "Little House" group, constituted themselves as a rump government and launched militias, armed, trained and choreographed well in advance, on a systematic massacre of Tutsis and moderate Hutus. Some Africa experts and human rights activists believe that France is quietly continuing to support the rump government. Journalist Frank Smyth, who has reported on French support for Rwanda for Human Rights Watch, noted in the *Village Voice* (5/17/94) that French officials received representatives of the murderous Little House government in late April.

It would not be the first time the French had stood by the Rwandan hardliners. In 1990, when the largely Tutsi Rwandan Patriotic Front (RPF) invaded from Uganda, France rushed to provide military support to the French-speaking Habiyarimana government. In February, when Hutu operatives killed about 1,000 people, Smyth told *Extra!*, the Clinton administration withheld its support from international efforts to pressure the Hutu hardliners that would have put the French on the hot seat. Washington's passivity, Smyth said, convinced the Hutu hardliners "that they could massacre all the Tutsis and Hutus willing to share power" and retain France's backing.

It is not as if French support for the Rwandan government was a great secret. Smyth's Human Rights Watch report, which clearly identified France as the Rwandan government's main foreign military backer, was widely distributed to the media in January 1994. Had the report not been ignored by the big media, says Smyth, it "could have been used to call into question France's policy of providing arms without conditionality" on the government's human rights practices.

Instead, even after the scope of the genocide was clear, France's role was obscured. French support for Habiyarimana was sometimes briefly mentioned—for example, in a *Washington Post* op-ed by Jennifer Parmelee (4/24/94), and in a *New York Times* article by Elaine Sciolino (4/15/94). But even in these references, French responsibility was played down—France "finds itself in the embarrassing position of having armed and advised the government that is now being accused of responsibility for many massacres," wrote Stephen Kinzer in the *New York Times* (5/25/94)—and mainstream journalists failed to explore the logical question of France's post-Habiyarimana role.

The Media Gloss Over U.S. Policy

But lack of interest about France is not surprising, given the media's complete lack of interest in U.S. policy. Pentagon documents show that since 1988, the U.S. has trained 29 Rwandan officers under the International Military Education and Training [IMET] program, and the 1995 IMET budget calls for training nine more. Human rights activists and some foreign media commentators have accused the Clinton administration of stalling UN Security Council efforts to intervene in Rwanda. Mainstream media reports have yet to focus on these issues.

Indeed, the operative principle seems to be don't-ask-don't-tell. An administration official, speaking on background, told *Extra!* that very few reporters had even bothered to ask whether

French troops on patrol pass members of the Hutu Interahamwe militia near Rwanda's border with Zaire on June 27, 1994. © Pascal Guyot/AFP/Getty Images.

Clinton's policy distinguished between the RPF rebels and the rump government. ("Human rights organizations and aid workers have uniformly held the Hutu-led militias responsible for most of the carnage in Rwanda," as Mark Fritz of the Associated Press reported—5/17/94.) Official administration policy, as expressed in mid-May after the military's role in killing hundreds of thousands was abundantly clear, is that the U.S. wants "both sides" to stop the fighting.

Such sanctimony has been challenged in regard to Bosnia, where persistent media reports pinpointed victim and aggressor—and spurred the Clinton administration to at least go through the motions of succoring the embattled Muslims. But, when it comes to Africa, wrote Elizabeth Schmidt in an op-ed in the *Baltimore Evening Sun* (5/10/94), "We don't demand—and we are not given—the careful historical context we expect in analysis of [European] 'ethnic conflicts.'"

Racist and Colonialist Views Pervade in the Media

Schmidt discusses the European colonists' preference for giving power and education to the lighter-skinned Tutsis and the bloody Hutu revolt against this dispensation after independence. "The roots of the Hutu-Tutsi rivalry must be considered in terms of the unequal distribution of power, privilege and economic resources that were clearly exacerbated, if not solely created, by European colonialism," Schmidt wrote.

Occasionally, reporters did serve up the political context of the genocide, but most often it was deeply buried. On May 5, the *New York Times* quoted the U.S. ambassador to Rwanda, David Rawson: "The ethnic dilemma was used by different sides as a shield behind which the play for power was being done. Quite clearly there was a real system to the political assassinations. There must be some system to the mass killings as well. It's not just mayhem."

Nevertheless, even after the politics behind the massacre was known, editors and reporters continued to prefer the Tarzan reruns imprinted in their minds. "Pure tribal enmity" (4/18/94) was *Time* magazine's explanation for the "tribal carnage" (4/25/94). The *San Francisco Chronicle* (5/7/94) and the *New York Post* (4/22/94) both made reference to Africa's "heart of darkness." Jennifer Parmelee (*Washington Post*, 4/24/94) was one of the few writers who stressed that "it is not as if Africans have any monopoly on armed madness."

Some, in their haste to shoehorn Rwanda into an ethnic framework, even got the ethnic distinctions wrong. In two successive issues (4/18/94, 4/25/94), *Time* incorrectly identified Prime Minister Agathe Uwilingyimana, a Hutu official who was slain by the military, as a Tutsi.

This latest variation on the "they-all-look-alike" theme, and the media's comfortable acceptance of the administration's "even-handed" policy, shows that to U.S. news elites, Africa and Africans' sufferings don't amount to a hill of beans . . . or a stack of bodies.

Many Women Perpetrated Genocide in Rwanda

Donna J. Maier

In the following viewpoint, the author provides extensive evidence of women's participation in genocidal attacks on Tutsis during the Rwandan genocide. She claims that it is unclear whether more women participated in Rwanda than in earlier genocides or whether there is simply more evidence of women's participation in Rwanda. In either case, the author asserts, acts of genocide by women suggest that women are not more peaceful than men, but rather that, given power, opportunity, and prejudice, they can behave as violently and cruelly as men during a genocide. She notes that some observers deny or excuse women perpetrators of genocide as exceptions to the rule, but she advises that justice can only be done when women, like men, are held fully accountable for their actions. Donna J. Maier is a professor of history at the University of Northern Iowa.

The role of women as perpetrators in the Rwanda Genocide has been documented much more so than that of women in other genocides and crimes against humanity: more than in the holocaust of World War II, than in the massacres of Mayan

Donna J. Maier, "Women Leaders in the Rwandan Genocide: When Women Choose to Kill," *Universitas*, vol. 8, 2012–2013. Copyright © 2012–2013 University of Northern Iowa. Reproduced by permission.

Guatemala's Indians in 1982, and more even than in the wide-spread atrocities that accompanied the break-up of the former Yugoslavia which were virtually concurrent with the Rwanda Genocide. It is not entirely clear why this is the case. Testimonies of women perpetrators and victims were collected in the immediate aftermath of the Rwandan Genocide by various human rights groups, most completely by the United Kingdom–based NGO [nongovernmental organization] African Rights which published its data within a year of the genocide. More evidence has emerged in the trials of genocidaires at the International Criminal Tribunal for Rwanda, and in trials in the national courts of Rwanda, Belgium, and other countries. These trials include the evidence of female victims, but also have included prosecution of high-level women perpetrators which have resulted in guilty verdicts.

Low-level violence and looting by women against one's neighbors is perhaps, sadly, unsurprising but the involvement of female leaders in the Rwanda genocide (cabinet officials, nuns, journalists, nurses, and teachers) is striking and factually well-established. Were women more likely to be perpetrators of genocide violence in Rwanda than in other cases of mass violence or does it appear this way only because we have more evidence? Regardless of the answer, this essay seeks to explore the evidence we do have of leading female perpetrators and their motivation. . . .

The Cultural Context of Female Perpetrators

Research on women in the genocide is scarcer than general analysis of the killings, though not non-existent, and what has been written has focused primarily on women victims whose survival stories are tragic and overwhelming. Their testimonies reinforce the shocking fact that killers and victims frequently were neighbors, but tell us little of the motivation of the killers. Scholars examining the general planning and propaganda climate preceding the genocide have documented a strong vein of gendered as well as ethnicized exhortation. Thus, while ethnic Tutsi were denounced both before and during the genocide as *inyenzi*—cockroaches—and filth, snakes and cannibals, Tutsi women were often especially singled out as vixens, temptresses and spies who had to be eliminated. The perception that Tutsi women were superior, more desirable, more beautiful than Hutu women, and also more haughty was a generalized cliché of pre-genocide Rwanda. For example, the propaganda newspaper *Kangura*, a major source of anti-Tutsi diatribes in pre-genocide Rwanda published the Hutu Ten Commandments in December 1990 which had as its first commandment:

1. Every Hutu should know that a Tutsi woman, whoever she is, works for the interest of her Tutsi ethnic group. As a result, we shall consider a traitor and Hutu who:
   - Marries a Tutsi woman
   - Befriends a Tutsi woman
   - Employs a Tutsi woman as a secretary or a concubine

Commandment 3 read:

3. Hutu women, be vigilant and try to bring your husbands, brother and sons back to reason.

And Commandment 7 read:

7. The Rwandan Armed Forces should be exclusively Hutu. The experience of the October 1990 was has taught us a lesson. No member of the military shall marry a Tutsi.

Furthermore, *Kangura* and other extreme Hutu publications made quite frequent use of pornographic cartoons which regularly depicted Tutsi women as traitorous seducers. . . . Thus, in the leadup to the genocide, Hutu were already encouraged to think of Tutsi women as well as men as the enemy and as targets for murder, with the added twist that Hutu women were encouraged to fear and hate Tutsi women. While this explains

A woman from the pro-government Hutu militia carries a machete in Gitarama, Rwanda, in a photo from June 13, 1994. © Alexander Joe/AFP/Getty Images.

some of the excessive male perpetrated sexual violence, sadism, and mutilation of Tutsi women that characterized the genocide, and the episodic participation of women in this sexual violence, I do not think it sufficient to explain the frequent enthusiastic wide-spread participation of Hutu women, and the leadership role some of them took, in the general killings.

Let us reiterate that in Rwandan society women were meant to be submissive to men and their place was in the home farming, cooking, house-keeping and child-rearing. Women were not even expected to be in the same room when men sat and talked about serious matters. Of course, as in all societies there were exceptions: In the 1890s, a famous Rwandan queen mother Kanjogera engineered a palace coup, organized the murder of the legitimate heir to the throne and his supporters, and then installed her own son as king in his place. In the 1990s, the Hutu wife of authoritarian President Habyarimana was widely considered to have more "backbone" than her husband, was sometimes known as "Kanjogera," and, although she fled to France three days after the genocide began, is viewed to this day as a major force behind planning the genocide. Women's roles were changing by the 1990s and many Rwandan women had received higher education and broken out of traditional occupational roles. There were nurses and teachers, nuns, even policewomen; some were medical doctors, several were parliamentarians, and the Minister of Justice, and the Minister of Women and Family Affairs were both women. Most significant was the Prime Minister of the transitional government from 1993–1994, Agathe Uwilingiyimana, a moderate Hutu woman who tried desperately to oversee a smooth peaceful transition to the power-sharing government agreed to in the Arusha Accords, and eventually elections. The genocide propaganda in those years never ceased to portray her in cartoons as a whore, literally naked in bed with other moderate politicians. She was savagely murdered and sexually mutilated within hours of the beginning of the genocide on the night of April 6, 1994. The genocide scholar Adam Jones even

suggests that the growing changes and tensions in gender relations in the 1990s, as women availed themselves more choice and
position in society

> may help to account not only for the lifting of "taboos" against
> the mass murder of women, but for Hutu women's conscrip-
> tion and (frequently) ready participation in the slaughter—a
> reflection in its macabre way, of women's greater independent
> agency in the Rwandan social equation. The added element of
> Hutu women's "subordination" to Tutsi women was doubtless
> a powerful motivation for the atrocities these Hutu women
> would inflict on other women.

Powerful Women in Leadership Positions

Examples in this paper of perpetrators of violence will be drawn
primarily from women who were leaders and in a position of
authority at the time of the genocide, and who thus had responsibility as superiors for the massacre, assault, rape, and killing of
thousands of people targeted for no other reason than that they
were of the Tutsi ethnic group. Sources presented here are primarily eye-witness statements and testimony given in the trials
of the ICTR [International Criminal Tribunal for Rwanda], and
survivor interviews taken by human rights organizations. ICTR
trial records also include judgment summaries of testimony, and
statements given in the Rwanda Courts system, Gacaca hearings,
and other national courts.

Pauline Nyiramasuhuko, Minster of Family Affairs and Women's Development

Let us begin with Pauline Nyiramasuhuko, a former social
worker, and the Minister of Family Affairs and Women's Development in the government of Rwanda during the genocide. After
the genocide she fled to DRC [Democratic Republic of Congo]
and then to Kenya where she was arrested in 1997. She was tried
at the ICTR and convicted on June 23, 2011 of genocide, con-

spiracy to commit genocide, extermination as a crime against humanity, rape as a crime against humanity, persecution as a crime against humanity, violence to life as a war crime, and outrages upon personal dignity as a war crime. She received a life sentence. Pauline was from the province of Butare, location of the National University of Rwanda, the only province of Rwanda with a Tutsi Prefet (governor), and a significant number of mixed Hutu-Tutsi marriages. The genocide killings had been underway for almost two weeks in Kigali and the rest of Rwanda but with no killings yet taking place in Butare when, on April 19 [1994], Pauline returned with the President Sindikubwabo and Prime Minister Jean Kambanda of the interim government to call upon the population of Butare to begin "the work" of killing Tutsi. The local Prefet, who had been trying to maintain calm in his province, was dismissed and killed shortly thereafter. The massacres then proceeded according to plan; the President and Prime Minister departed, while Pauline stayed on in her home town and supervised much of the genocide killings there:

> Apart from indoctrinating [the people] Pauline took care of the logistics for the militiamen who came in from Kigalito set fire on Butare. She distributed grenades and supplied the petrol for the burning down of houses in the rural areas and distributed machete and other useful equipment to the assassins.

On April 24 Tutsi were ordered to assemble in the local stadium where they were promised food and shelter, but instead Pauline organized the Interahamwe [militia] under the leadership of her son, Shalome, surrounded the stadium and massacred the thousands inside, mostly hacked to death with machetes. The court found Pauline guilty of ordering militiamen to rape Tutsi women before they killed them and she herself aided and abetted these rapes. She also ordered her men to take gasoline from her own car to burn alive a group of raped women, from which one woman witness survived, later to testify. Pauline continued to supervise the progress of the genocide for the next two months, until the RPF army reached and liberated Butare. During those months she set up a road-block in front of her house where any person caught who looked Tutsi, or tried to use a false identity card, was killed. As elsewhere in Rwanda, Tutsis took refuge in churches, schools, hospitals, swamps, and on top of hills, where they were nevertheless attacked and killed by thousands. Some Tutsi took refuge in the local government office in Butare town and here at first they found some shelter. But Pauline, angry that they were protected there, visited the prefecture office regularly, ordering as many as would fit into a pick-up truck each night to be taken away, raped, tortured, and killed. One witness, a Tutsi woman who had survived into mid-May because "she didn't look Tutsi" recounted:

> During my brief stay at the prefecture [offices] I saw Nyirama-suhuko take out Tutsis to kill many times. She said we weren't human beings. On the contrary she said we were dirt. . . . She came with a group of high ranking Interahamwe militiamen. She stayed beside the van and always gave them orders.

Pauline would later deny that she had anything to do with killings, insisting to a BBC reporter that "It was the Tutsi who massacred the Hutus" and appealing to traditional gender assumptions: "I am ready to talk to the person who says I could have killed. I cannot even kill a chicken. If there is a person who says that a woman, a mother, killed then I'll confront that person. . . ." But the evidence presented at her trial said otherwise. Regarding the nightly abduction, rape and murder of refugees from the prefecture office, the judges convicting Pauline noted that the evidence was "among the worst encountered by this Chamber; it paints a clear picture of unfathomable depravity and sadism."

Witnesses testified that she ordered the Interahamwe and public through a megaphone, that "it was necessary to kill the Inyenzi [including] foetus or old person." In mid-June, even as the RPF were closing in on Butare, Pauline still continued her supervisions of the killings. Another witness testified:

In the night of the same day [in mid-June] the famous Pauline Nyiramasuhuko accompanied by her Interahamwe, including her son Chalome, arrived. The van stopped and right there, in full view was Nyiramasuhuko in black uniform. . . . I saw it all. She stayed by the van and ordered the militiamen to "hurry up." She said it in a loud voice. That's when the militiamen started the selection. They took . . . Mbasha's wife who [said] "Have pity have pity on my children" and I clearly remember Nyiramasuhuko saying "Kill her quickly." . . . There was also another Tutsi girl called Triphine. When the interahamwe went to take her she cried out in a loud voice, "save me save me." Nyiramasuhuko said "Don't take long, slit her throat."

Agnes Ntamabyariro, Minister of Justice

Agnes Ntamabyariro was a highly educated lawyer and Minister of Justice in the Rwanda government, before and during the genocide. She at one time directed an NGO that raised micro-finance loans for poor Rwandan women, though Jacqueline Novogratz, who worked with her at the time suspected her of embezzling funds. She came from the prefecture of Kibuye and during the genocide organized the militia there, distributed weapons, drew up lists of Tutsi to be killed, and gave incendiary speeches in order to encourage the killings. As Minister of Justice, she authorized the murder of the Tutsi Prefet of Butare mentioned above. She is said to have been particularly determined in the later weeks of the genocide to have the Tutsi wives of Hutu men exterminated. Witnesses stated that she exhorted with megaphone speeches to the peoples of her area to work harder at killing, criticizing them for "contenting themselves with killing only a few old women" and telling them that "When you begin extermination, nothing, no one must be forgiven." And this was in May 1994, after about a quarter million Tutsi had already been killed in the province! Her driver, Gervais Ngendahayo, testified at her trial that after inspecting Tutsi corpses at the roadblocks, she distributed rewards to the killers. Agnes was eventually arrested in Zambia where

The Catholic Church and the Rwandan Genocide

One of the most troubling aspects of the genocide [is] the role of some church leaders in the genocide. The simple fact of a Catholic population committing such atrocities is worrisome. But a handful of priests and nuns also participated in the genocide. It is not hard to find stories of heroism among church leaders—clergy who died with their flocks, nuns who hid Tutsis—but it is just as easy to find evidence of church leaders who killed.

Fr. Athanase Seromba's story is inescapable. Fr. Seromba was convicted of genocide and extermination by the United Nations International Criminal Tribunal for Rwanda in December 2006 and is currently serving a fifteen-year sentence. The clergyman encouraged two thousand of his Tutsi parishioners to seek refuge in the church and then ordered a bulldozer to demolish the building. All inside were crushed. The rubble has been left undisturbed as a genocide memorial.

We also cannot ignore the actions of Sisters Gertrude Mukangango and Maria Kizito, two Benedictine nuns convicted by a Belgian court in 2001 for participating in the massacre of over five thousand Tutsis seeking refuge at the Sovu convent in Butare, Rwanda. Sister Gertrude and Sister Maria are currently serving fifteen- and twelve-year sentences respectively. The two provided fuel to militias who burned some of the refugees alive. They also coaxed victims to come out of hiding where they could be slaughtered out in the open. Sister Gertrude, superior of the convent, ordered Tutsi sisters hiding other Tutsis to produce those hidden in exchange for their own lives.

Jeffry Odell Korgen, "Forgiving the Unforgivable: Peacebuilding in Rwanda," in Solidarity Will Transform the World. *Maryknoll, NY: Orbis, 2007, p. 119.*

she had fled. She was tried in Kigali, the only member of the Genocide government to be tried in Rwanda, the rest being tried in Arusha [Tanzania]. In 2009 she was given a life sentence....

Lesser Leaders

The examples given here so far are high profile women, leaders, planners, and enablers, the people who, like many male ringleaders of the genocide, never actually took up a machete and killed, who "kept their fingernails clean." There were of course other less high profile female perpetrators. There was Rose Karushara "The Butcher of Kimisagara," a local leader in the ruling political party in Kigali. Everyone described her as a huge powerful woman who could beat up men before she would order them killed in front of her house. She held meetings with interahamwe, distributed arms, and visited roadblocks where she decided who would be killed and who spared. "At least five thousand people were killed, all thrown into the Nyabarongo river under orders from Karushara ... as paper is thrown into the dustbin." There was Zainabu Mukundufite who in the indictment of her husband is said to have "headed a female group of Interahamwe.... This group was notorious for sexually torturing Tutsi women before killing them. The group forced iron rods into the genitals of the Tutsi women. They also asked Tutsi women to produce milk from their bodies if they were Tutsi.... Those Tutsi women were then tortured to death."...

Beyond these examples, we know that at the grassroots, groups of women ululated men into action at the massacres and sang their praises for their successes at killing, looted the stacks of corpses, often finished off the dying, and supplied beer and food to the Interahamwe at the roadblocks and massacre sights. They identified Tutsi neighbors for the Interahamwe to kill, and shouted out hiding Tutsi children in the sugar cane fields. In fact the Holocaust scholar Adam Jones maintains that "the extensive role of women in perpetrating the Rwandan genocide is apparently without parallel in recorded history."

Women Perpetrators Should Be Held Accountable

What then should we make of women perpetrators of the geno-cide? Does the phenomenon require a different analysis beyond conventional efforts to account for the horror of genocide and mass murder, both in Rwanda and around the world? Some de-fense lawyers and even Rwandan judges tend to insist that it was an aberration for women to have participated in the genocide. Since women and mothers are not expected to do such things, they *could not* have done such things as women, and therefore are not genuine women but deviants. The female perpetrators are thus depicted as anomalies and monsters, and so placed outside our ability to comprehend human, especially female behavior. This is a dangerous historical/analytical approach when thinking of both male and female perpetrators—though it is sometimes done (with similar obfuscating consequences) in cases of male extremists such as [Russian dictator Joseph] Stalin or [Cambo-dian dictator] Pol Pot. If we demonize women perpetrators, re-garding them as aberrant and unnatural, then we separate them, and fail to confront the motives and context of their actions, de-nying or excusing them, and thus we will never achieve justice for victims or deter future mass killings.

Similarly some defense lawyers, and perpetrators them-selves, insist that women simply could not do such awful things and therefore they *did not* do these things: the perpetrators have been falsely accused, badly misunderstood, or were powerless to say no. As Sara Brown, observer of the U.S. genocide/deporta-tion trial of Beatrice Munyenyezi (daughter-in-law of Pauline Nyiramasuhuko) notes, "The woman-as-mother narrative is, at its core, an essentialist belief that a woman who is also a mother cannot perpetrate crimes during genocide because she is just that—a woman and a mother. . . . [Munyenyezi's] defense did not provide any other reasons." Carrie Sperling has masterfully demonstrated how news accounts feed this discourse as they re-port on the dress, hairstyle and "nice aunt" appearance of female perpetrators, particularly in the case of Nyiramasuhuko, who for example was described as wearing to court a "green flowery dress one day, a pressed cream-colored skirt and blouse set the next." Even some Rwandan NGO women organizations maintain that "Women have a different nature to men. They are not violent. . . . If there had been more women in power, the genocide would not have taken place." It is an essentialist argument also made by some Western feminist theorists who posit "that men are inherently more warlike than women. . . . The wars we have suffered are the result of male-dominated political and military systems."

This essentialism simply is not supported by the witness testimony, survivor accounts, and mounting judicial evidence that there were women with authority in Rwanda who abused power as readily as men. Jacqueline Novogratz worked with Agnes Ntamabyariro in women's development before the genocide, and interviewed her in prison after the genocide. Distressed by this former Minister of Justice's total lack of remorse and openly expressed enduring ethnic hatred, Novogratz commented:

> Many individuals believe that if women ruled the world we'd finally have a chance at peace. While that may be true, Agnes stood as a reminder that power corrupts on an equal-opportunity basis.

Novogratz believed that Agnes had been led astray by a desire for power: "Agnes loved the trappings of power and when all was said and done she'd traded integrity and whatever good she'd built." On the other hand, [researcher Nicole] Hogg observed that many of the women she interviewed in prison insisted that they had no power to say no: "I am really surprised they put me in the first category [of criminal charges], I am a woman. . . . I had no power." Were the women in the examples given in this paper powerless to say no to men? Such an argument is not unlike that of male perpetrators who protest in their trials that they were coerced or forced against their better judgment to participate in the killings. When applied to women it not only discounts their intelligence and skills, but provides a mechanism for dissociating women from the personal responsibility of choice and decision making. Not all Hutu women participated in the violence of the genocide, nor did all men. All were surrounded by pressures and years of socializing propaganda that dehumanized Tutsi and anyone who befriended them, yet many chose not to succumb to it, and not to participate in the genocide, although too many of those were not "left to tell the story." The moderate Hutu prime minister Agathe Uwilingiyimana who heroically lost her life in the cause of peace and toleration is the most striking but hardly unique example.

Nevertheless, disturbingly, but ultimately not surprisingly, many women, both humble and powerful, deliberately chose to embrace the genocidal ideology of hate and violence, and even chose to participate with enthusiasm and dedication. Excusing or exoticizing, even sensationalizing women's genocidal crimes on the grounds that they are outside our, or Rwandan, gender norms of female behavior diverts us from the pursuit of explaining, understanding, and preventing future genocidal actions. A binarized gender-based analysis of female perpetrators reinforces and perpetuates a patriarchal myth that women by their very nature are implausible agents of atrocities. Instead the evidence is plentiful that when women are provided an atmosphere of positive incentives and impunity similar to those of men, as Jones notes, "their degree of participation in genocide and the violence and cruelty they exhibit runs closely parallel to their male counterparts" and for similar motives.

Men Were Singled Out for Gendercide in Rwanda

Adam Jones

The author of the following viewpoint argues that much of the killing in the Rwandan genocide was targeted at men—it was "gendercidal," or aimed at eliminating one gender as well as one ethnic group. Tutsi men were generally singled out and killed, while Tutsi women were raped, tortured, and sometimes kept as sexual slaves, according to the viewpoint. The author emphasizes that these general patterns were not followed in all cases; many women and girls were also killed during the genocide. He adds that Tutsi reprisals against Hutus following the genocide also tended to focus on killing men. Adam Jones is an associate professor of political science at the University of British Columbia Okanagan in Kelowna, British Columbia, Canada, executive director of Gendercide Watch, and an editor for the Journal of Genocide Research.

The genocide in the tiny Central African country of Rwanda was one of the most intensive killing campaigns—possibly the *most* intensive—in human history. Few people realize, however, that the genocide included a marked gendercidal component [that is, one gender was targeted for death]; it was predominantly or overwhelmingly Tutsi and moderate Hutu males who were targeted by the perpetrators of the mass slaughter. The gender-cidal pattern was also evident in the reprisal killings carried out by the Tutsi-led RPF [Rwandan Patriotic Front] guerrillas during and after the holocaust. . . .

Men Were the Main Target of Killings

The gender dimension of the killings is one of the least-known and least-investigated aspects of the Rwanda genocide. But an increasing number of sources have acknowledged, with [political sociologist] Ronit Lentin, that "Throughout the genocide, it was Tutsi men who were the primary target." [Consultant and author] Judy El-Bushra writes that

> During the war of 1994, and particularly as a result of the geno-cidal massacres which precipitated it, it was principally the men of the targeted populations who lost their lives or fled to other countries in fear. . . . This targeting of men for slaughter was not confined to adults: boys were similarly decimated, raising the possibility that the demographic imbalance will continue for generations. Large numbers of women also lost their lives; however, mutilation and rape were the principal strategies used against women, and these did not necessarily result in death.

The trend had been evident throughout the 1990–94 period, when numerous smaller-scale massacres of Tutsis took place, and when, according to Human Rights Watch and other observers, Tutsi males were targeted almost exclusively, as presumed or "potential" members of the RPF guerrilla force.

There are strong indications that the gendering of the Rwandan genocide evolved between April and June 1994, with adult males targeted almost exclusively before the genocide and predominantly in its early stages, but with more children and women swept up in the later stages. . . . In a comprehensive 1999 report on the genocide, [historian and human rights activist] Alison Des Forges wrote:

CHANGE IN SEX RATIO IN GIKONGORO PREFECTURE, RWANDA		
Commune	Sex ratio in 1990	Sex ratio in 2002
Karama	93.2	87.0
Karambo	91.1	89.3
Kinyamakara	93.8	90.0
Kivu	85.5	93.9
Mubuga	93.4	83.6
Mudasomwa	90.7	89.9
Muko	100.8	86.1
Musange	96.1	88.6
Musebeya	87.6	91.0
Nshili	92.8	88.2
Nyamagabe	91.3	87.7
Rukondo	95.4	88.9
Rwamiko	92.5	81.5
Gikongoro Prefecture	92.5	88.6

Note: Sex ratio is the number of males per 100 females in the population.

Source: Marijke Verpoorten, "The Death Toll of the Rwandan Genocide: A Detailed Analysis for Gikongoro Province," *Population*, vol. 60, no 4, 2005, p. 20.

In the past Rwandans had not usually killed women in conflicts and at the beginning of the genocide assailants often spared them. When militia had wanted to kill women during an attack in Kigali in late April, for example, Renzaho [a principal leader of the genocide] had intervened to stop it. Killers in Gikongoro told a woman that she was safe because "Sex has no ethnic group." The number of attacks against women [from mid-May onwards], all at about the same time, indicates that a decision to kill women had been made at the national level and was being implemented in local communities.

Women Suffered Extreme Violence

It must be stressed that if such a new stage of killing can indeed be isolated, this does not mean that women and girls were immune to mass murder until that point. Although the number of women actually killed was substantially lower than the number of murdered men, many women (along with girl children) were massacred from the outset. They were also exposed to a wide range of horrific (if generally non-fatal) abuses. Notes Human Rights Watch:

> Testimonies from survivors confirm that rape was extremely widespread and that thousands of women were individually raped, gang-raped, raped with objects such as sharpened sticks or gun barrels, held in sexual slavery (either collectively or through forced "marriage") or sexually mutilated. These crimes were frequently part of a pattern in which Tutsi women were raped after they had witnessed the torture and killings of their relatives and the destruction and looting of their homes. According to witnesses, many women were killed immediately after being raped. Other women managed to survive, only to be told that they were being allowed to live so that they would "die of sadness." Often women were subjected to sexual slavery and held collectively by a militia group or were singled out by one militia man, at checkpoints or other sites where people were being maimed or slaughtered, and held for personal sexual service. The militiamen would force women to submit sexually with threats that they would be killed if they refused. These forced "marriages," as this form of sexual slavery is often called in Rwanda, lasted for anywhere from a few days to the duration of the genocide, and in some cases longer. Rapes were sometimes followed by sexual mutilation, including mutilation of the vagina and pelvic area with machetes, knives, sticks, boiling water, and in one case, acid.

A Tutsi man shows the scars on his face and head from attacks he endured during the Rwandan genocide. © Scott Peterson/Liaison/Getty Images.

Rwanda may in fact stand as the paradigmatic example of "genocidal rape," owing to the fact that many of the Tutsi women who were gang-raped have subsequently tested positive for the HIV virus. According to the UK *Guardian*, "rape was a weapon of genocide as brutal as the machete." "I was raped by so many interahamwe [militia members] and soldiers that I lost count," said one survivor, Olive Uwera. "I was in hospital for a year afterwards. A few months after my child was born the doctors told me I was HIV-positive." Tests conducted on the 25,000 Tutsi women members of the Widows of Genocide organisation (Avega) showed that "two-thirds were found to be HIV-positive.... Soon there will be tens of thousands of children who have lost their fathers to the machete and their mothers to AIDS."

Reprisal Killings of Hutus Singled Out Men

As soon as the genocide broke out, the Tutsi-led RPF launched a concerted drive on Kigali, crushing Rwandan government resistance and bringing a halt to the genocide in successive areas of the country. RPF forces based in Kigali also took up arms, and succeeded in protecting a large number of residents from the holocaust. On July 4, 1994, Kigali fell to the RPF, and the genocide and "war" finally came to an end on July 18. There followed a massive flight of Hutus to neighboring countries, notably to refugee camps in Zaire [now the Democratic Republic of the Congo], as well as large-scale reprisals against Hutus who were alleged to have participated in the holocaust. Most of these reprisal killings also had strong gendercidal overtones. For example, in the town of Mututu, according to Human Rights Watch (*Leave None to Tell the Story*):

> RPF soldiers asked children to go bring back the adults in their families who were hiding in the fields and bush. On June 10, after several hundred adults had returned, the soldiers directed them to assemble at the commercial center to be transported to a safer location to the east. The RPF reportedly killed a number of young men at the market place late in the afternoon and tied up some of the others. The crowd was directed to set out for the commune, about one hour away by foot. The soldiers reportedly killed some men on the way and threw their bodies in latrines or in a compost heap at a reservoir. In another report from the same area, witnesses said that RPF soldiers and armed civilians gathered men and adolescent boys at the home of a man named Rutekereza and then killed them.

In another case, a witness reported that "I saw the RPF soldiers bringing bodies in trucks at night and throwing them in toilets at Mwogo, near where they had dug their trenches. They brought men already wounded with their arms tied behind their backs. They brought no women." Various other incidents cited by the Human Rights Watch investigators attest to the broad gendercidal pattern. In other instances, however, "The [RPF] soldiers killed without regard to age, sex, or ethnic group." The organization cites sources to the effect that between 25,000 and 45,000 Hutus were killed in all, though other estimates are higher.

Rwanda in Retrospect

Alan J. Kuperman

The following viewpoint argues that once the genocide in Rwanda began, the West could have done little to prevent it. Western nations had little warning of the genocide and could not have sent troops to Rwanda fast enough and in large enough numbers to prevent the bulk of the killings, according to the viewpoint. The author writes that threats of Western intervention alone would not have slowed killing and may even have spurred the Hutu government to redouble its genocidal efforts. The author believes that Western nations could have prevented the genocide if they had put more troops on the ground before the events began. The lesson from Rwanda, he concludes, is that international players must focus on careful diplomacy in global trouble spots in order to anticipate and prevent such atrocities in the future. Alan J. Kuperman is a MacArthur transnational security fellow at the MIT Center for International Studies.

Several years after mass killings in Bosnia, Somalia, and Rwanda, the United States is still searching for a comprehensive policy to address deadly communal conflicts. Among

Washington policymakers and pundits, only two basic principles have achieved some consensus. First, U.S. ground troops generally should not be used in humanitarian interventions during ongoing civil wars. Second, an exception should be made for cases of genocide, especially where intervention can succeed at low cost. Support for intervention to stop genocide is voiced across most of the political spectrum.

Despite this amorphous consensus that the United States can and should do more when the next genocide occurs, there has been little hard thinking about just what that would entail or accomplish. A close examination of what a realistic U.S. military intervention could have achieved in the last clear case of genocide this decade, Rwanda, finds insupportable the oft-repeated claim that 5,000 troops deployed at the outset of the killing in April 1994 could have prevented the genocide. This claim was originally made by the U.N.'s commanding general in Rwanda during the genocide and has since been endorsed by members of Congress, human rights groups, and a distinguished panel of the Carnegie Commission on Preventing Deadly Conflict. Although some lives could have been saved by intervention of any size at any point during the genocide, the hard truth is that even a large force deployed immediately upon reports of attempted genocide would not have been able to save even half the ultimate victims. . . .

The Knowledge Gap

Although U.S. intelligence reports from the period of the genocide remain classified, they probably mirrored those of the international news media, human rights organizations, and the U.N.—because U.S. intelligence agencies committed virtually no in-country resources to what was considered a tiny state in a region of little strategic value. During the genocide's early phases, the U.S. government actually received most of its information from nongovernmental organizations. A comprehensive review of such international reporting—by American, British, French,

Belgian, and Rwandan media, leading human rights groups, and U.N. officials—strongly suggests that President Clinton could not have known that a nationwide genocide was under way in Rwanda until about April 20. . . .

Potential U.S. Interventions

In retrospect, three levels of potential U.S. military intervention warrant analysis: maximum, moderate, and minimal. None would have entailed full-blown nationwide policing or long-term nation-building by American troops. Based on historical experience, full-blown policing would have required some 80,000 to 160,000 personnel—that is, ten to twenty troops per thousand of population—an amount far more than logistically or politically feasible. Nation-building would have been left to a follow-on multinational force, presumably under U.N. authorization.

Maximum intervention would have used all feasible force to halt large-scale killing and military conflict throughout Rwanda. Moderate intervention would have sought to halt some large-scale killing without deploying troops to areas of ongoing civil war, in order to reduce U.S. casualties. Minimal intervention would have relied on air power alone.

A maximum intervention would have required deployment of a force roughly the size of one U.S. division—three brigades and supporting units, comprising about 15,000 troops and their equipment—with rules of engagement permitting the use of deadly force to protect endangered Rwandans. After establishing a base of operations at Kigali airport, the force would have focused on three primary goals: halting armed combat and interposing itself between FAR and RPF forces on the two stationary fronts of the civil war; establishing order in the capital; and finally fanning out to halt large-scale genocidal killing in the countryside. None of these tasks would have been especially difficult or dangerous for properly configured and supported American troops once they were in Rwanda. But transporting such a force 10,000 miles to a landlocked country with limited airfields would have been considerably slower than some retro-spective appraisals have suggested.

The first brigade to arrive would have been responsible for Ki-gali: coercing the FAR and RPF to halt hostilities, interposing itself between them, and policing the capital. The second brigade would have deployed one battalion in the north to halt the civil war in Ruhengeri and another as a rapid-reaction force in case American troops drew fire. The third brigade, supplemented by a battalion of the second brigade, would have been devoted to halting the killing in the countryside. Such an effort would have required roughly 2,000 troops to halt the war in Kigali, 3,000 to police Kigali, 1,000 to stop the fighting in the north, 1,500 for a rapid-reaction force, and 6,000 to stop the genocide outside Kigali—a total of about 13,500 troops, in addition to support personnel.

The time required to deploy such a force would have de-pended mainly on its weight. A division-size task force built around one brigade each from the 101st Air Assault, 82nd Air-borne, and a light army division can be approximated as the av-erage of those divisions—26,550 tons, including 200 helicopters and 13,500 personnel. (The Marines could also have substituted for the one of the brigades.) Because Rwanda is a landlocked country in Central Africa, and because speed is critical in stop-ping a genocide, the entire force would have been airlifted. The rate of airlift would have been constrained by factors such as the delay in loading planes at U.S. bases, excessive demand for air refueling, fuel shortages in Central Africa, and the limited air-field capacity in Kigali and at the potential staging base at En-tebbe in neighboring Uganda. At an optimistic rate of 800 tons daily, the task force would have required 33 days to airlift. Per-sonnel, which are much quicker to transport than their cargo, could have been sent first—but it would have been imprudent to deploy them into the field without sufficient equipment and logistics. Several additional days would also have been required for the delay between the deployment order and start of airlift, for the gradual increase in the capacity of theater airfields unaccustomed to such traffic, and for travel to and unloading at the theater. In addition, the rate of force deployment might have been slowed by the need to use limited airlift capacity for food, medicine, and spare parts to sustain the first troops to arrive. Thus the entire force could not have closed in the theater until about 40 days after the president's order.

Advance units, however, could have begun operations much sooner. Approximately four days after the order, a battalion or two of Army Rangers could have parachuted in and seized Kigali airport at night. Follow-on troops could have expanded outward from the airfield to establish a secure operating base. Within about two weeks, sufficient troops and equipment could have arrived to halt the fighting, form a buffer between the FAR and the RPF in Kigali and northwest Rwanda, and fully police the capital. Only later, however, could the intervention force have turned in earnest to stopping the genocide in the countryside as helicopters, vehicles, and troops arrived.

Some observers have suggested that the genocide would have ceased spontaneously throughout Rwanda upon the arrival of Western enforcement troops in Kigali—or possibly even earlier, upon the mere announcement of a deployment. They claim that the extremists would have halted killing in hopes of avoiding punishment. But these Hutu were already guilty of genocide and could not have imagined that stopping midway would gain them absolution. More likely, the announcement of Western intervention would have accelerated the killing as extremists tried to finish the job and eliminate witnesses while they had a chance. Such was the trend ahead of the RPA advance, as Hutu militias attempted to wipe out remaining Tutsi before the rebels arrived. During the genocide, the ringleaders even trumpeted false reports of an impending Western intervention to help motivate Hutu to complete the killings. Although the Hutu generally held back from mass killing at sites guarded by foreigners to avoid provoking Western intervention, they would have lost this incentive for restraint had such an intervention been announced.

The 6,000 U.S. troops deployed to the countryside would have been insufficient to establish a full police presence, but they could have found and protected significant concentrations of threatened Rwandans. Ideally, helicopter reconnaissance could have identified vulnerable or hostile groups from the air and then directed rapid response forces to disperse hostile factions and secure the sites. Alternately, ground troops could have radiated out from Kigali in a methodical occupation of the countryside. Displaced Rwandans could have been gathered gradually into perhaps 20 large camps for their protection.

Depending on the search method, large-scale genocide could have been stopped during the fourth or fifth week after the deployment order, by May 15 to May 25. Interestingly enough, this would have been before the task force's airlift had been completed. Based on the genocide's progression, such an intervention would have saved about 275,000 Tutsi, instead of the 150,000 who actually survived. Maximum credible intervention thus could not have prevented the genocide, as is sometimes claimed, but it could have spared about 125,000 Tutsi from death, some 25 percent of the ultimate toll. . . .

A Western Failure of Will?

Many observers have claimed that timely intervention would have prevented the genocide. Some even asserted at first that UNAMIR itself could have done so, although most now acknowledge that the peacekeepers lacked sufficient arms, equipment, and supplies. Conventional wisdom still holds that 5,000 well-armed reinforcements could have prevented the genocide had they been deployed promptly when the killing began—and that the West's failure to stop the slaughter resulted exclusively from a lack of will. Rigorous scrutiny of six prominent variations of this assertion, however, finds all but one dubious.

Human Rights Watch makes the boldest claim: Diplomatic intervention could have averted the genocide without additional military deployment. These advocates contend that a threat from the international community to halt aid to any Rwandan government that committed genocide would have emboldened Hutu moderates to face down the extremists and extinguish violence. As proof, they note that moderate FAR officers appealed for support from Western embassies during the first days of violence, and that the intensity of massacres waned after the West intensified its condemnations in late April.

However, this argument ignores the fact that virtually all of Rwanda's elite military units were controlled by extremist Hutu, led by Colonel Theoneste Bagosora. These forces demonstrated their power and ruthlessness by killing Rwanda's top political moderates during the first two days of violence. By contrast, moderate Hutu officers had virtually no troops at their disposal. The moderates avoided challenging the extremists not because of a lack of Western rhetorical support but because of mortal fear for themselves and their families. This fear was justified given that the extremists stamped out any nascent opposition throughout the genocide—coercing and bribing moderate politicians, removing them from office or killing them if they did not yield, shipping moderate soldiers to the battlefront, and executing civilian opponents of genocide as "accomplices" of the rebels. The decline in massacres in late April is explained simply by the dwindling number of Tutsi still alive. International condemnation did little except compel extremists to try harder to hide the killing and disguise their rhetoric. Even these superficial gestures were directed mainly at persuading France to renew its military support for the anti-Tutsi war—hardly an indication of moderation.

The only way that the army's Hutu moderates could have reduced the killing of Tutsi civilians would have been to join forces with the Tutsi rebels to defeat the Hutu extremists. This was militarily feasible, given that the Tutsi rebels alone defeated both the FAR and the Hutu militias in just three months—but it was politically implausible. By April, Rwanda had already been severely polarized along ethnic lines by four years of civil war, the calculated efforts of propagandists, and the October 1993 massacre of Hutu by Tutsi in neighboring Burundi. Even moderate Hutu politicians once allied with the rebels had come to fear Tutsi hegemony. Although the moderate Hutu officers sincerely favored a cease-fire and a halt to the genocide, they could not realistically have defected to the Tutsi rebels—at least until the FAR's defeat became imminent.

The second claim is that 5,000 U.N. troops deployed immediately upon the outbreak of violence could have prevented the genocide. But this assertion is problematic on three grounds. It assumes such troops could have been deployed virtually overnight. In reality, even a U.S. light-infantry ready brigade would have required about a week after receiving orders to begin significant operations in the theater and several more days for all its equipment to arrive. Further delays would have resulted from reinforcing the brigade with heavy armor or helicopters, or from assembling a multinational force. Even if ordered on April 10, as requested at the time by Dallaire, reinforcements probably could not have begun major operations to stop genocide much before April 20. Moreover, it is unrealistic to argue that urgent intervention should have been launched on April 10—given that the international community did not realize genocide was under way until at least ten days later.

Intervention advocates, such as the Carnegie Commission, also erroneously characterize the progression of the genocide. The commission claims that there was a "window of opportunity from about April 7 to April 21" when intervention "could have stemmed the violence in and around the capital [and] prevented its spread to the countryside." In reality, killing started almost immediately in most of Rwanda, and by April 21, the last day of this purported "window," half the ultimate Tutsi victims already were dead. Even if reinforcements had arrived overnight in Kigali, Dallaire was unaware of genocide outside the capital and thus would not have deployed troops to the countryside in time to prevent the massacres.

Furthermore, 5,000 troops would have been insufficient to stop genocide without running risks of failure or high casualties. Only 1,000 troops would have been available for policing Kigali—some three troops per thousand residents, which is grossly inadequate for a city in the throes of genocide. In the countryside, U.S. commanders would have faced a stark choice: either concentrate forces for effective action, leaving most of the country engulfed in killing; or spread forces thin, leaving troops vulnerable to attack. To avoid such painful choices in the past, U.S. military planners have insisted on deploying more than 20,000 troops for interventions in the Dominican Republic, Panama, and Haiti—all countries with populations smaller than Rwanda's.

A third claim is that U.N. headquarters had three months' advance notice of genocide and could have averted the killing simply by authorizing raids on weapons caches. Critics cite the so-called genocide fax—a January 11, 1994, cable from Dallaire to U.N. headquarters in New York that conveyed a Hutu informant's warning that extremists were planning to provoke civil war, kill Belgian peacekeepers to spur their withdrawal, and slaughter the Tutsi with an Interahamwe militia of 1,700 troops that the informant was training. The cable also reported an arms cache containing at least 135 weapons, which Dallaire wanted to seize within 36 hours.

Dallaire, however, raised doubts about the informant's credibility in this cable, stating that he had "certain reservations on the suddenness of the change of heart of the informant. Possibility of a trap not fully excluded, as this may be a set-up." Raising further doubt, the cable was the first and last from Dallaire containing such accusations, according to U.N. officials. Erroneous warnings of coups and assassinations are not uncommon during civil wars. U.N. officials were prudent to direct Dallaire to confirm the allegations with Habyarimana himself, based on the informant's belief that "the president does not have full control over all elements of his old party/faction." Dallaire never reported any confirmation of the plot. . . .

A fourth claim holds that quickly jamming or destroying Hutu radio transmitters when the violence broke out could have prevented the genocide. A Belgian peacekeeper who monitored broadcasts testified, "I am convinced that, if we had managed to liquidate [Radio Mille Collines], we could perhaps have avoided, or in any case limited, the genocide." A human rights advocate characterized the jamming as "the one action that, in retrospect, might have done the most to save Rwandan lives." But radio broadcasts were not essential to perpetuating or directing the killing. By April, Rwandans had been sharply polarized along ethnic lines by civil war, propaganda, and recent massacres in Burundi. Habyarimana's assassination was a sufficient trigger for many extremist Hutu to begin killing. Moderate Hutu were usually swayed not by radio broadcasts but by threats and physical intimidation from extremist authorities. Furthermore, orchestration of the genocide relied not merely on radio broadcasts but on the government's separate military communications network. Silencing the radio might have had most impact prior to the genocide, when broadcasts were fostering polarization, but such action would have been rejected at the time as a violation of sovereignty. Even if hate radio had been preventively extinguished, the extremists possessed and used other means to foster hatred.

The fifth variant of the intervention argument is that the Western forces sent to evacuate foreign nationals during the first week could have restored order in Kigali—and thereby prevented the genocide had they merely been given the orders to do so. Just four days after Habyarimana's assassination, some 1,000 lightly armed Western evacuation troops, mainly French and Belgian soldiers, had arrived in Kigali, where Belgium's 400-troop UNAMIR contingent was already stationed. Another 1,100 reserves were less than two hours away by air. But it is doubtful that this small force, lacking the right equipment or logistical support, could have quickly quashed violence in the capital—or that doing so would have stopped the genocide elsewhere. The Western evacuators had to commit half their force to guarding the airport at the town's outskirts and a few key assembly points, leaving few available for combat. In addition, coordinated action would have been inhibited by the widespread perception that France and Belgium sympathized with opposite sides in the civil war. Moreover, Kigali was defended by 2,000 elite Rwandan army troops and several thousand regulars equipped with heavy weapons, another 2,000 armed fighters of the Hutu militia, and 1,000 national police. Also located there were more than 1,000 Tutsi rebels who had access to surface-to-air missiles and had explicitly threatened to attack the evacuators if they extended their mission. Even if the small Western force had somehow halted the violence in Kigali, it lacked the equipment and logistics to deploy troops quickly to the countryside. Rural killing probably would have continued unless the ringleaders were captured and coerced to call off the slaughter. Such a search would not have been a quick or simple matter for any force, as demonstrated by the failed search for the Somali warlord Mohamed Farah Aidid by U.S. troops in 1993. Ill-equipped evacuation troops could have wasted weeks looking for the ringleaders while genocide continued at a torrid pace in the countryside, where 95 percent of Rwandans lived.

The sixth claim is most realistic: Had UNAMIR been reinforced several months prior to the outbreak of violence, as Belgium urged at the time, genocide might have been averted. More troops with the proper equipment, a broad mandate, and robust rules of engagement could have deterred the outbreak of killing or at least snuffed it out early. Such reinforcement would have required about 3,500 additional high-quality troops in Kigali, armored personnel carriers, helicopters, adequate logistics, and the authorization to use force to seize weapons and ensure security without consulting Rwandan police. This would have been the 5,000-troop force that Dallaire envisioned—but one deployed prior to the genocide.

Under the U.N.'s peacekeeping rules, Rwanda's government would have had to consent to such a change—and probably would have. Prior to the genocide, its cabinet still was dominated by the

Hutu opposition moderates who had negotiated the Arusha accords, which called for a neutral international force to "guarantee [the] overall security of the country." The U.N. Security Council had watered down implementation of this provision, authorizing UNAMIR only to "contribute to the security of the city of Kigali." As tensions mounted in early 1994, the Rwandan government again asked the U.N. to dismantle armed groups, but the peacekeepers were too weak. Belgium pleaded for reinforcements and a new mandate from the Security Council in January and February 1994 on the grounds that UNAMIR could not maintain order. But the United States and Britain blocked this initiative before it could even reach a vote, citing the costs of more troops and the danger that expanding the mission could endanger peacekeepers—as had occurred in Somalia the previous October.

The Rwandan government, however, almost certainly would have welcomed a reinforcement of UNAMIR prior to the genocide. Five thousand troops in the capital would have meant 16 troops for every thousand Rwandans, a ratio historically sufficient to quell severe civil disorders. Such a force might well have deterred the genocide plot. Failing that, well-equipped peacekeepers could have protected moderate Hutu leaders and Tutsi in the capital and captured some of the extremists during the first days of violence, thereby diminishing the chance of large-scale massacres in the countryside. Indeed, such early reinforcement of UNAMIR is the only proposed action that would have had a good chance of averting the genocide.

Lessons

The most obvious lesson of Rwanda's tragedy is that intervention is no substitute for prevention. Although the 1994 genocide represents a particularly tough case for intervention in some respects—such as its rapid killing and inaccessible location— it would have been a relatively easy mission in other respects, including the limited strength of potential opponents. Yet even an ideal intervention in Rwanda would have left hundreds of thousands of Tutsi dead. To avert such violence over the long term, there is no alternative to the time-consuming business of diplomacy and negotiation. Tragically, international diplomatic efforts in Rwanda prior to the genocide were ill conceived and counterproductive.

Whether pursuing prevention or intervention, policymakers must use their imagination to better anticipate the behavior of foreign actors. In Rwanda, Western officials failed to foresee the genocide, despite numerous warning signs, in part because the act was so immoral that it was difficult to picture. Increased awareness of such risks demands that any peacekeeping force deployed preventively to a fragile area be adequately sized and equipped to stop incipient violence—rather than be sent as a lightly armed tripwire that serves mainly to foster a false sense of security. If the West is unwilling to deploy such robust forces in advance, it must refrain from coercive diplomacy aimed at compelling rulers to surrender power overnight. Otherwise, such rulers may feel so threatened by the prospect of losing power that they opt for genocide or ethnic cleansing instead. Western diplomacy that relies mainly on the threat of economic sanctions or bombing has provoked a tragic backlash not just in Rwanda, but also in Kosovo and East Timor over the last few years as local rulers opted to inflict massive violence rather than hand over power or territory to lifelong enemies. In each case, Western military intervention arrived too late to prevent the widespread atrocities.

International Intervention Could Have Prevented the Rwandan Genocide

Gregory H. Stanton

The author of the following viewpoint argues that the United Nations, the United States, and other Western nations had sufficient evidence that genocide was imminent in Rwanda. However, he argues, they did not want to intervene and refused to acknowledge or heed the warning signs. The author writes that a commitment by Western powers to increase UN forces in Rwanda, or a willingness to use the forces already in place, could have prevented large numbers of deaths and substantially reduced the scale of the genocide. Gregory H. Stanton is a research professor in genocide studies and prevention at George Mason University in Fairfax, Virginia.

In 1994, 500,000 to one million Rwandan Tutsis along with thousands of moderate Hutus, were murdered in the clearest case of genocide since the Holocaust. The world withdrew and watched. To borrow a Biblical metaphor, we passed by on the other side. [Academic and author] Samantha Power, in her searing article in the *Atlantic Monthly*, "Bystanders to Genocide: Why the United States Let the Rwandan Tragedy Happen," and in her book, *A Problem From Hell: America and the Age of*

Genocide, says "The story of U.S. policy during the genocide in Rwanda is not a story of willful complicity with evil. U.S. officials did not sit around and conspire to allow genocide to happen. But whatever their convictions about 'never again,' many of them did sit around, and they most certainly did allow genocide to happen." Ms. Power concludes that her extensive research, including interviews with most of the U.S. policy makers who made the decisions, "reveals that the U.S. government knew enough about the genocide early on to save lives, but passed up countless opportunities to intervene."

Early Warnings Were Ignored

There were plenty of "early warnings" of the Rwandan genocide, but they were systematically ignored. The best book on the Rwandan genocide, [investigative journalist] Linda Melvern's superb *A People Betrayed: The Role of the West in Rwanda's Genocide* sets them forth in detail. To list just a few, in the spring of 1992, the Belgian ambassador in Kigali, Johan Swinner warned his government that the Akazu, a secret group of Hutu Power advocates organized around the President's wife, "is planning the extermination of the Tutsi of Rwanda to resolve once and for all, in their own way, the ethnic problem. . . ." In October 1992, Professor Filip Reyntjens organized a press conference in the Belgian Senate in which he described how Hutu Power death squads were operating and named their leaders, including Colonel Théoneste Bagosora, who later coordinated the genocide. In March 1993, four human rights groups led by Human Rights Watch and the International Federation of Human Rights issued a report on mass killings in Rwanda. Although the word "genocide" was excised from the final report, the press release announcing it, written by Canadian law professor William Schabas, used the word genocide to describe the mass killings of Tutsis. The U.N. Special Rapporteur on Summary, Arbitrary, and Extrajudicial Executions, René Dégni-Ségui, conducted a mission to Rwanda in April 1993 and reported to the U.N. Human Rights Commission in August 1993 that the trial massacres of Tutsis, already begun by then, constituted genocide under the Genocide Convention.

During the months prior to the Rwandan genocide, General Roméo Dallaire, commander of the U.N. Assistance Mission in Rwanda (UNAMIR), warned the U.N. Department of Peace-keeping Operations (DPKO) that Hutu extremists were planning a campaign to exterminate Tutsis. In a now famous cable to New York on January 11, 1994, which DPKO authorized him to share with the U.S., French and Belgian Embassies, General Dallaire asked for authority to search for and seize the caches of machetes and other weapons that had been shipped into Rwanda for the Hutu militias, the Interahamwe. Iqbal Riza, deputy to then Un-dersecretary General for Peacekeeping Kofi Annan, in a letter signed by Annan, denied him permission to act, as exceeding UNAMIR's mandate, and instructed him instead to take the information to the Rwandan government, many of whose members were planning the genocide. DPKO's refusal to authorize action was confirmed on January 14 by [U.N.] Secretary General [Boutros] Boutros-Ghali himself.

General Dallaire's early warning of genocide was corroborated by the assassinations and further trial massacres of January to March 1994, which were also reported in cables to the U.S. State and Defense Departments. On January 21–22, UNAMIR seized a planeload of Belgian arms (shipped on a French plane) purchased by the Rwandan Armed Forces, which were then kept in joint UNAMIR/Rwandan government custody. At the request of DPKO, Dallaire provided confirmation of arms shipments and was finally authorized by the DPKO on February 3, 1994 to "assist the government of Rwanda" in recovering illegal arms. In mid-February, the Rwandan Minister of Defense requested landing authorization for three planes carrying arms, but General Dallaire refused. On February 27, General Dallaire repeated his request to DPKO for authorization to seize the caches of weapons the Interahamwe [Hutu] militias had hidden all over Rwanda. (General Dallaire had sent a Senegalese UNAMIR soldier to see some of the arms caches with his own eyes.) But U.N. authorities, including his direct superior, Canadian General Maurice Baril, again refused, referring privately to General Dallaire as a "cowboy."

Belgium explicitly warned the U.N. Secretary General of impending genocide on February 25, 1994, but Belgium's plea for a stronger U.N. peacekeeping force was rebuffed by members of the U.N. Security Council, particularly the U.S. and the United Kingdom. . . .

U.S. Officials Refused to Acknowledge Genocide

Dr. Alan Kuperman, in his recently published book, *The Limits of Humanitarian Intervention: Genocide in Rwanda,* challenges "the common wisdom" that simple political will could have stopped the Rwandan genocide. He argues that well-meaning mediations and dilatory promises to back them up (e.g. the Arusha peace agreement on Rwanda) can actually increase the likelihood of genocide as they threaten the interests of ruling groups. He takes aim particularly at those who blame the U.S. for its inaction after the Rwandan genocide began. The U.S. and United Kingdom played the leading role at the U.N. Security Council during the genocide. Dr. Kuperman argues that neither U.S. nor U.K. policy makers recognized the killings as genocide for at least three weeks, and that even if they had acted immediately thereafter, it would have taken three more weeks to send in U.S. reinforcements. He says that by that time, three-quarters of the killing was done.

Although the U.S. Defense Intelligence Agency (D.I.A.) recognized from radio intercepts as early as April 7 that centrally organized mass killing of Tutsis was underway, D.I.A. warnings went unheeded in the American government. Some U.S. diplomats in Kigali began calling the killings genocide on the same, first day, and directly communicated their views to the State Department in Washington, DC. The U.S. Embassy's Deputy Chief of Mission Joyce Leader has told me personally that she began using the word genocide in her daily telephone calls to the State Department from the start. It was clear to her that the Interahamwe and Presidential Guard were committing genocide. Dr. Kuperman questions whether Leader's reports and the D.I.A. warnings were shared with top officials of the State and Defense Departments and the National Security Council. The answer is that although these reports were shared with top officials, including Assistant Secretaries and other policy makers, at their daily interagency secure teleconferences about the Rwandan catastrophe, other reports from the U.S. Ambassador to Rwanda and the C.I.A. contradicted them. Dr. Kuperman observes that although reports of the mass killing quickly reached mid-level officers in the U.S. State and Defense departments, the surfeit of information served to cloud rather than clarify the situation.

Why did policy makers at the State Department and National Security Council refuse to recognize that genocide was underway in Rwanda? There are probably two reasons, both compelled by a prevenient group decision to avoid U.S. involvement.

First, the facts were resisted. The U.S. government was forewarned of the impending genocide. Communications were sent by cable, e-mail, and secure telephone from the U.S. embassy in Kigali informing the State Department about General Dallaire's premonitions months before April 6. But in 1993, President Clinton had ordered U.S. forces withdrawn from Somalia after General Aideed's militia (possibly trained by Osama bin Laden's Al Qaeda) killed eighteen Army Rangers. Policy makers in Washington, D.C., especially Anthony Lake, Dick Clarke and Susan Rice at the National Security Council, George Ward at the State Department, and the Joint Chiefs of Staff at the Defense Department, distrusted U.N. peacekeeping missions and did not want the U.S. to get involved in another African "civil war," another "quagmire." In response to Somalia, President Clinton had just signed Presidential Decision Directive 25, which the same policy makers had drafted, limiting U.S. involvement in U.N. peacekeeping operations. But it specifically allowed such inter-

General Roméo Dallaire (right), commander of the UN Assistance Mission in Rwanda (UNAMIR), speaks to the press in Rwanda on April 15, 1994. Dallaire's requests for an increased mandate and troop reinforcements were not honored by the UN Security Council. © Scott Peterson/Liaison/Getty Images.

vention in cases of "genocide." They therefore resisted the "cognitive dissonance" of reports of impending genocide in Rwanda, which might have created at least a moral duty to intervene. The anti-interventionists dismissed General Dallaire's reports as "unconfirmed," meaning that U.S. embassy staff or intelligence personnel had not independently written about the arms caches and reported them through official cable channels. They utilized cable reports from the American ambassador, David Rawson, in the early days of the genocide, to argue that this was just another episode of bi-lateral civil war, not a one-sided genocide. Ambassador Rawson had grown up in Burundi with the Tutsi-Hutu conflict and he spoke Kirundi, the language of Burundi, which is closely related to Kinyarwanda, the language of Rwanda. The Ambassador's appraisal of the violence, however confused, therefore carried considerable credibility. After the entire U.S. mission left for Burundi on April 10, with Ambassador Rawson in the last car, no further official channels existed to "confirm" reports from Kigali. The first defense against action was denial of the facts.

The second reason for inaction was legal malpractice. The State Department Bureau of African Affairs asked the State Department Legal Advisor's office whether the massacres constituted genocide. On April 26, Carl Pendorff issued an intelligence estimate calling the Rwandan massacres genocide. At a crucial interagency meeting called by Deputy Assistant Secretary of State Prudence Bushnell, she asked, "Is this genocide? And if it is, what are we going to do about it?" Ms. Joan Donoghue of the Legal Advisors Office gave her opinion that the word genocide should be avoided, because she questioned whether the killings possessed the requisite "intent" and because use of the G-word, "genocide," would obligate the U.S. to take action to stop it. Her oral opinion was soon followed by a written opinion from the Legal Advisor saying the same things. Sadly, the lawyers were wrong on both points. Intent can be proven by direct statements, but it is more often inferred from actions, like the systematic pattern of killing of Tutsis in Rwanda. And unfortunately, the Genocide Convention imposes no legal requirement to take action to stop a genocide. It only requires passage of national legislation to outlaw genocide, and prosecution or extradition of suspected perpetrators. The Convention's Article 8 states, "Contracting Parties may call upon the competent organs of the U.N." to take action to suppress a genocide. But that is not legally required.

Recognition Comes Too Late

For over two months, the Legal Advisors told the American government not to call the Rwandan killings genocide. The State Department ordered the U.S. mission at the U.N. to vigorously oppose use of the term. The U.K. rewrote a Presidential Statement proposed on April 29 by New Zealand's Colin Keating, that month's President of the Security Council, to avoid use of the word. On May 4, the U.N. Secretary General declared a "real genocide."

The U.S. continued to avoid the G-word until June. In a now infamous press conference on June 10, State Department press spokesperson Christine Shelley, reading from talking points prepared by the Legal Advisors, declared that "acts of genocide have occurred in Rwanda." But when pressed by a reporter, she was unprepared to call it "genocide." This false distinction was finally buried the same day by Secretary of State Warren Christopher, himself a lawyer, who knew that Article 2 of the Genocide Convention defines genocide as acts of genocide. An act of genocide is genocide, just as an act of rape is rape, or an act of murder, murder. The U.S. Secretary of State finally called it genocide on June 10, after most of the killing was over.

State Department lawyers and policy makers did not want to use the G-word because they wanted to avoid a duty to act. So they chose another name for what was happening in Rwanda, one that would result in non-intervention: "civil war." Civil wars are two-sided (or multi-sided.) The lesson the Clinton Administration learned from Somalia was, "Don't get involved in African civil wars." Policy makers, including U.S. Ambassador David Rawson in Kigali, saw the killing as a continuation of the civil war that had plagued Rwanda since 1990, a war the Arusha Accords were supposed to settle. What they missed was the turn toward genocide of the Hutu Power movement. Because they did not know much about genocide, they ignored the fact that most genocides have been committed during wars, including civil wars. Robert Melson has shown in Revolution and Genocide that it is precisely during wars that pariah groups are most likely to become identified as threats, and therefore objects of genocide. Genocide and civil war are correlative, not mutually exclusive. The second defense against action was legal definitionalism—denial that mass murder fit the legal definition of genocide.

The press and human rights groups also failed to name the crime until two weeks into the genocide. French newspapers were an exception. The first newspaper that called it genocide was *Libération* in an article by Jean-Philippe Ceppi on April 11, 1994. *Libération* had also been the first to use the word "genocide" in an early warning article about death squads in Rwanda in February 1993. But the left-wing *Libération* is not given much weight by French foreign policy makers, and is not read by anyone in Washington. *Le Monde* followed with a story by Jean Hélène on April 12. It, too, was ignored. Human rights groups held back until Ken Roth, Executive Director of Human Rights Watch, wrote Colin Keating, President of the U.N. Security Council on April 19. The Pope waited to call it genocide until April 27.

Besides the mis-reporting of the Rwandan killing as civil war, Dr. Kuperman notes that other factors contributed to inaction: "Second, after a few days, violence was reported to be on the wane when in reality it was accelerating. Third, most early death counts were gross underestimates, sometimes by a factor of ten. . . . Fourth, the initial focus was almost exclusively on Kigali, a relatively small city, and failed to note the broader scope of the violence.

U.S. and U.K. Reluctance Prevents Meaningful U.N. Action

The U.N. did not wait to intervene in Rwanda until the beginning of the genocide. Acting under Chapter VI of the U.N. Charter, the U.N. Department of Peacekeeping Operations had deployed 2,539 U.N. Assistance Mission in Rwanda (UNAMIR) troops to Rwanda by April 6, 1994. Dr. Kuperman claims they were too lightly armed to deter the Rwandan genocidists, who he says numbered 100,000, including the heavily armed Presidential Guard. He agrees with General Dallaire that UNAMIR needed heavier weapons, full deployment of its 2,548 authorized troops plus an equal number of reinforcements, all of them well-trained and well-supplied, with a clear mandate giving them authority to forcefully stop killing. That could have been written into U.N. Security Council resolution 872 that created UNAMIR. But the U.S. and U.K. had opposed a robust mandate with the 4,500 troops recommended by General Dallaire because it would have been too expensive.

When the genocide began, policy makers in Washington and at the U.N. believed that UNAMIR forces lacked the strength to arrest the spread of the conflagration, and they refused to consider sending in their own troops. In U.S. government parlance, that was a "non-starter." When that word is used, it really means, "We don't want to think about it." It is the product of what social scientists have called "groupthink." Those who dissent are afraid to step forward to challenge the group assumptions. State Department policy makers who attended a crucial meeting in the International Organization Affairs bureau on UNAMIR's future have told me that after Assistant Secretary of State for African Affairs George Moose, National Security Council Peacekeeping Advisor Susan Rice, and International Organizations Deputy Assistant Secretary George Ward had all agreed that UNAMIR could not fulfill its mandate and should be withdrawn, they felt as subordinates that they could not object or contradict them. They did not consider changing UNAMIR's mandate because they assumed that troop-contributors had only committed to a peacekeeping operation, not an operation to stop genocide. No one suggested asking the troop-contributors if they would stay. No one suggested sending in U.S. troops. The U.N. Security Council's earlier failure, because of U.S. and U.K. reluctance, to send a strong UNAMIR force created the self-fulfilling prophecy that nothing effective could be done.

In the U.N. Security Council, the U.S. took an active stance against keeping the UNAMIR troops in Rwanda. Ambassador Karl Inderfurth announced that position on April 15 in "Informals", closed meetings of the Security Council, with the representative of the genocidal Rwandan regime present. Ambassador Inderfurth's announcement of U.S. policy had fatal consequences. The next day, the Rwandan Interim Government met, and knowing it could now act with impunity, decided to extend the genocide to Southern Rwanda.

In the first week of the genocide, General Dallaire asked for a change in UNAMIR's mandate that would authorize him to take action to stop as much killing as possible. But instead, on April 21, the Security Council, led by the U.S. and the U.K., ordered reduction of UNAMIR to a token force of 270 troops. Over five hundred thousand Rwandan Tutsis were murdered while the U.N. "did a Pontius Pilate," as General Dallaire told State Department officials in Fall 1994.

UNAMIR Intervention Could Have Saved Lives

Dr. Kuperman states, "Indeed, by my calculations, three-quarters of the Tutsi victims would have died even if the West had launched a maximum intervention immediately upon learning that a nationwide genocide was being attempted in Rwanda." He concludes that although intervention during the Rwandan genocide would have been less effective than some think, saving 125,000 lives would have justified maximal intervention. He notes that even the belated, minimal response proposed in May 1994 by the U.S., which would have unrealistically expected Tutsis to walk through militia-infested areas to reach "safe zones" outside Rwanda might have saved 75,000 lives. (The cruel fate awaiting people who relied on weakly defended U.N. "safe areas" was demonstrated a year later in Srebenica, Bosnia.)

How many lives could have been saved? We will never know. But General Dallaire, the commander on the ground who knew the situation best, was and still is, convinced that a robust UNAMIR mandate plus reinforcements, demonstrating the international political will to stop further genocide, could have saved hundreds of thousands of lives.

Dr. Kuperman argues that reinforcements could not have arrived in time to save most victims' lives. But he only considers U.S. troops sent from the continental U.S.A. as reinforcements, a strangely self-defeating concept for a U.N. peacekeeping force. Perhaps the most telling refutation of his view is the fact that over 1,000 heavily armed French and Belgian troops flew into

Kigali by April 10 to evacuate their own nationals. If they had, instead, been used to reinforce UNAMIR, they might have had a powerful effect in deterring the spread of the genocide. An additional 500 Belgian reserves were available in Kenya, and 800 more French troops were stationed in central Africa. Two hundred and fifty U.S. Special Operations troops stood by in Burundi to assist, if necessary, with the evacuation of U.S. citizens. There were also tens of thousands of U.S. troops stationed in Europe, the Persian Gulf, the Indian Ocean, and other places much closer to Rwanda than the continental U.S.A.

Even without these reinforcements, according to General Dallaire, the UNAMIR troops could have used the weapons they had, which were superior to the machetes of the Interahamwe, to take down the roadblocks by force, and protect Tutsis who had gathered in defensible places. The fact that the remaining 456 UNAMIR peacekeepers were able to save at least 25,000 lives by guarding people who had gathered in churches, stadiums, and hotels, leaves the question open whether the full 2,500 member force could not have saved many more lives had the U.N. Security Council immediately mandated it to do so. In places protected by the 456 UNAMIR volunteers who stayed, most people survived. Even against the better-armed Presidential Guard, a robust response by UNAMIR might have deterred plans to extend the genocide. International outrage at attacks on U.N. peacekeepers might have also helped forge the political will necessary to obtain reinforcements. Instead the U.N. Security Council, led by the U.S. and the U.K. decided to cut and run. As General Dallaire later told State Department officials, "A peacekeeping force that is trying to stop genocide must expect to take casualties, or it is worthless."

The major problem from the beginning of UNAMIR was that all but one of the Western powers were unwilling to send troops to intervene, or even to provide airlift and financing for an international force. The result was that poorly trained troops from Bangladesh, lacking any equipment, were the largest contingent, followed by the Ghanaians, who arrived without a single vehicle. The Belgian force numbered only 420, and withdrew within days after the massacre of ten Belgian soldiers guarding the Prime Minister. The attack was consciously planned to drive out the Belgians. The Hutu Power militants had learned the lessons of Somalia, too. If you kill them, they will leave. . . .

Genocide Denial Was Intentional and Deadly

The major Western governments did know from the first days that mass killing was underway. The U.S. Deputy Chief of Mission used the word genocide in her calls to the State Department from the beginning. Much of the communication was done by secure phone calls, since both Joyce Leader and Ambassador Rawson were cut off from access to the U.S. Embassy for long periods. Classified documents confirm this very early recognition of mass killing. The information did reach the top levels of government.

The real problem was genocide denial, first through denial of the facts, and then through denial that the mass murder was genocide. State Department and Defense Department lawyers who were opposed to intervention, either because of their own views or to please their anti-interventionist superiors, denied that the mass murders constituted genocide. That this denial was intentional can be seen from the fact that they continued to deny the genocide for two months, until long after it was obvious to nearly everyone else that one of the worst genocides of the twentieth century was underway. . . .

The Rwandan genocide could have been prevented. The early warning signs were clear. UNAMIR troops were already on the ground in Rwanda, though with inadequate training and material support. But in a failure of political will, the U.S., the U.K., the U.N. Secretariat and the U.N. Security Council refused to act to prevent or stop the genocide. At least 500,000 people perished. . . .

Although the U.S. and U.K. were willing to commit billions to save lives in Bosnia, where people are white, and the war was close to the interests of the European community, they were unwilling to do so in Rwanda, where people are black, and neither country has strategic or economic interests. This racist double standard was pointed out repeatedly by Nigeria's Ambassador Gambari in the U.N. Security Council. Our circle of moral concern excluded people of a different race in a continent far away. We ignored our common humanity.

CHAPTER 3

Personal Narratives

Chapter Exercises

1. Writing Prompt

Imagine that you are a Tutsi survivor of the genocide who has returned to live in your hometown in Rwanda. Describe your experiences during the genocide and what life is like in Rwanda following the genocide. Consider whether it is important for you to forgive those who killed your friends or family members, and why.

2. Group Activity

In small discussion groups, come up with a set of recommended actions for the current Tutsi-led government of Rwanda to implement to prevent another genocide from occurring in Rwanda in the future. In making its recommendations, the group should take into account political and ethnic issues that were unresolved following the Tutsi-led takeover of Rwanda in July 1994.

A Genocide Survivor and Her Attacker Share Their Stories

Jason Straziuso

In the following viewpoint, a reporter interviews a Hutu man and a Tutsi woman who work together for an organization that helps genocide survivors in Rwanda. According to the author, the man was a member of his church's choir before the genocide began, but when violence broke out he was asked to kill Tutsis and he obliged. Among his victims was Alice Mukarurinda, the Tutsi woman he now works with, the author writes. During the genocide, he killed her baby, and badly wounded her, according to the author. The two discuss how they have reconciled and address their fears that denial of the genocide by some Hutus may lead to more violence in the future. Jason Straziuso is the East Africa bureau chief for the Associated Press.

S he lost her baby daughter and her right hand to a manic killing spree. He wielded the machete that took both.

Yet today [April 2014], despite coming from opposite sides of an unspeakable shared past, Alice Mukarurinda and Emmanuel Ndayisaba are friends. She is the treasurer and he the vice president of a group that builds simple brick houses for genocide survivors. They live near each other and shop at the same market.

Twenty Years Ago Feels Like Yesterday

Their story of ethnic violence, extreme guilt and, to some degree, reconciliation is the story of Rwanda today, 20 years after its Hutu majority killed more than 1 million Tutsis and moderate Hutus. The Rwandan government is still accused by human rights groups of holding an iron grip on power, stifling dissent and killing political opponents. But even critics give President Paul Kagame credit for leading the country toward a peace that seemed all but impossible two decades ago.

"Whenever I look at my arm I remember what happened," said Alice, a mother of five with a deep scar on her left temple where Emanuel sliced her with a machete. As she speaks,

Alice Mukarurinda (left) and Emmanuel Ndayisaba pose outside of Alice's house in Nyamata, Rwanda, in March 2014. © AP Images/Ben Curtis.

Emmanuel—the man who killed her baby—sits close enough that his left hand and her right stump sometimes touch.

On Monday [April 7, 2014], Rwanda marks the 20th anniversary of the beginning of 100 days of bloody mayhem. But the genocide was really in the making for decades, fueled by hate speech, discrimination, propaganda and the training of death squads. Hutus had come to resent Tutsis for their greater wealth and what they saw as oppressive rule.

Rwanda is the most densely populated country in mainland Africa, slightly smaller than the U.S. state of Maryland but with a population of more than 12 million. The countryside is lush green, filled with uncountable numbers of banana trees.

The Hutu-Tutsi divide may be the country's most notorious characteristic but also its most confounding. The two groups are so closely related that it's nearly impossible for an outsider to tell which the average Rwandan belongs to. Even Rwandans have trouble knowing who is who, especially after two decades of a government push to create a single Rwandan identity.

For Alice, a Tutsi, the genocide began in 1992, when her family took refuge in a church for a week. Hutu community leaders began importing machetes. Houses were burned, cars taken.

Hutu leaders created lists of prominent or educated Tutsis targeted for killing. They also held meetings where they told those in attendance how evil the Tutsis were. Like many of his Hutu neighbors, Emmanuel soaked in the message.

A Church Choir Singer Learns to Kill

The situation caught fire on April 6, 1994, when the plane carrying Rwanda's president was shot down. Hutus started killing Tutsis, who ran for their lives and flooded Alice's village.

Three days later, local Hutu leaders told Emmanuel, then 23, that they had a job for him.

They took him to a Tutsi home and ordered him to use his machete. A Christian who sang in his church choir, Emmanuel had never killed before. But inside this house he murdered 14 people. The next day, April 12, Emmanuel found a Tutsi doctor in hiding and killed him, too. The day after, he killed two women and a child.

"The very first family I killed, I felt bad, but then I got used to it," he says. "Given how we were told that the Tutsis were evil, after the first family I just felt like I was killing our enemies."

In the meantime, Alice's family took refuge in a church, just as they had done before, crammed in with hundreds of others. But this time, Hutu attackers threw a bomb inside and set the church on fire. Those who fled the fire inside died by machetes outside. Alice lost some 26 family members, among the estimated 5,000 victims at the church.

Alice, then 25, escaped with her 9-month-old daughter and a 9-year-old niece into Rwanda's green countryside, moving, hiding, moving. She hid in a forested swamp.

"There were so many bodies all over the place," she says. "Hutus would wake up in the morning and go hunting for Tutsis to kill."

By late April rebel Tutsi fighters led by Kagame had reached the capital and chased Hutus out. Hutu troops began to flee to neighboring countries, and the violence spread, with killings carried out by both sides.

Emmanuel Attacks Alice and Leaves Her for Dead

On April 29, Emmanuel joined Hutu soldiers searching the countryside for Tutsis. The attackers blew a whistle whenever they found a Tutsi hiding.

The murders began at 10 A.M. and lasted until 3 P.M. Alice had been hiding in a swamp for days, keeping out only the top of her face so she could breathe. That was where the Hutus found her.

They surrounded the swamp. Then they attacked.

First they killed the girls. When that was done, they came after Alice. She was sure she would die, but instinctively put up her arm to defend herself.

Emmanuel, Alice's school mate, recognized the woman but couldn't recall her name. Perhaps that made it easier to rain down machete blows on Alice's right arm, severing it just above the wrist. He sliced her face. His colleague pierced a spear through her left shoulder.

They left her for dead.

She was bloodied, scarred, and missing a hand, yes, but not dead. Alice fell unconscious, she says, and was found three days later by other survivors. It was only then that she realized she no longer had a right hand.

In the months after the genocide, guilt gnawed away at Emmanuel. He saw his victims during nightmares. In 1996, he turned himself in and confessed.

His prison term lasted from 1997 until 2003, when Kagame pardoned Hutus who admitted their guilt. After he was freed, he began asking family members of his victims for forgiveness. He joined a group of genocide killers and survivors called Ukurrkuganze, who still meet weekly.

Forgiveness Is Possible

It was there that he saw Alice, the woman he thought he had killed.

At first he avoided her. Eventually he kneeled before her and asked for forgiveness. After two weeks of thought and long discussions with her husband, she said yes.

"We had attended workshops and trainings and our hearts were kind of free, and I found it easy to forgive," she says. "The Bible says you should forgive and you will also be forgiven."

Josephine Munyeli is the director of peace and reconciliation programs in Rwanda for World Vision, a U.S.–based aid group. A survivor of the genocide herself, Munyeli says more killers and victims would like to reconcile but many don't know who they attacked or were attacked by.

"Forgiveness is possible. It's common here," she says. "Guilt is heavy. When one realizes how heavy it is the first thing they do to recuperate themselves is apologize."

Although Rwanda has made significant progress since the genocide, ethnic tensions remain. Alice worries that some genocide planners were never caught, and that messages denying the genocide still filter into the country from Hutus living abroad. She believes remembrance is important to ensure that another genocide never happens.

For Emmanuel, the anniversary periods bring back the nightmares. He looks like a man serving penance, who does not want to talk but feels he must.

"I've been asking myself why I acted like a fool, listening to such words, that this person is bad and that person is bad," Emmanuel says. "The same people that encouraged the genocide are the ones saying there was no genocide."

He, too, worries that the embers of the genocide still smolder.

"The problem is still there," Emmanuel says. "There are Hutus who hate me for telling the truth. There are those up until now who participated in the genocide who deny they took part."

A Musician Remembers His Escape from the Rwandan Genocide

Nicola Luksic

The author of the following viewpoint interviews Jean Paul Samputu, a Rwandan Tutsi musician who fled Rwanda before the genocide. During the genocide, his family was killed by Hutus, the author reports, and one of the killers was Samputu's best friend. Samputu says he spent nine years struggling with grief, which led to addiction and violence. He eventually decided he needed to forgive his friend in order to move on with his life. The two of them reconciled and began speaking publicly about their experience in an effort to aid reconciliation efforts in Rwanda. Nicola Luksic is a producer at CBC/Radio-Canada.

Rwandan musician Jean Paul Samputu realizes that it is hard for most people to understand how he can forgive his childhood friend for killing his family.

"But for me, when I came to forgive him, it was like I won," said Samputu, who is now based in England. "It's the right thing to do because we cannot continue hating each other. We have children who follow us and if we don't give them a good education in love, another genocide will happen."

Nicola Luksic, "Rwanda Genocide: Why Jean Paul Samputu Forgives His Family's Murderer," CBC News, April 9, 2014. www.CBC.ca. Copyright © 2014 CBC. Reproduced by permission.

There are millions of genocide survivors with stories similar to Samputu's, but it is often the case that the trauma consumes them for life.

"People like Jean Paul who've suffered unspeakable circumstances don't always recover," said Payam Akhavan, a law professor at McGill University who also served as the first legal advisor to the prosecutor's office of the International Criminal Tribunals for the former Yugoslavia and Rwanda at The Hague [Netherlands].

"There are many survivors who are broken for life, but his is a story that gives us hope because somehow he found redemption through forgiveness."

Escaping Rwanda Before the Genocide

Samputu's family is Tutsi. He grew up believing that there wasn't any difference between Hutus and Tutsis. But in 1991 he was rounded up with other Tutsis and put in jail for six months as the anti-Tutsi campaign began to mount.

As soon as he was released from prison, his father encouraged Samputu to flee Rwanda. He reluctantly left his village behind, reassured that his friend Vincent would keep an eye on his father and the family.

Samputu was in Uganda when the genocide erupted on April 6, 1994. Over the course of the next 100 days nearly a million people were brutally slaughtered—among them Samputu's mother, father, three brothers and a sister.

"I lost my mind," said Samputu. "Every day I drank to forget. It was like I was in hell. I wanted to kill Vincent, and since I couldn't kill Vincent I started to kill myself."

On July 20, 1994, Samputu made his way back to his home village and found his family's house empty. He soon found out from his neighbours that his friend Vincent had killed his father and was among those responsible for killing his family.

He moved to Kigali and then back to Uganda. His drinking and drug use got in the way of his music career—he says he would

Musician Jean Paul Samputu, a survivor of the genocide in Rwanda, performs at the All Nations Peace Concert in Bethlehem, Pennsylvania, in 2007. © AP Images/The Express-Times/Joe Gill.

show up for gigs but would be so intoxicated he couldn't get up on stage. Samputu soon found himself in and out of prison for provoking fights and not paying bills at hotels and bars.

"It took nine years dealing with anger, bitterness and resentment," said Samputu. "I realized I couldn't continue. By being angry, I couldn't bring back my family."

Setting an Example for Others

Samputu cut himself off from drugs and alcohol [and] took a meditation retreat where he spent three months in prayer and relative silence. He came to the conclusion that the only way for him to move forward with his life is to reach out to Vincent and forgive him.

In 2007 he went back to his village and spoke at the gacaca (a traditional court) where he met Vincent and publicly forgave him.

"Just as the victim of genocide suffers, so does the perpetrator," said McGill University's Akhavan. "This doesn't mean that the person is not criminally responsible, but it is a negation of the humanity of the perpetrator to take another human's life."

Samputu and Vincent spent the next few years speaking publicly about their reconciliation in hopes that it would inspire other Rwandans to do the same.

Vincent is now living in Kampala. He initially agreed to do an interview with the CBC Radio program Ideas, but declined at the last minute citing concerns for his safety, as he doesn't want anyone in Kampala to know about his past.

"People often [think] that forgiveness is a gift to the offender. But forgiveness is for you, not for the offender," said Samputu, acknowledging it was difficult to convince many Rwandans of his decision.

Akhavan agrees forgiveness post-genocide is a way for a victim to come to terms with the horror they faced and that is a personal choice. But beyond the individual level, he says the international community must place emphasis [on] identifying the symptoms of a pending genocide and acting on it. It's the machinery behind human atrocity that must be identified and shut down, he says.

"People don't pick up machetes overnight and start killing the father of their best friend," said Akhavan who was commissioned by the UN to investigate and report on its failure in Rwanda. "It takes effort to make people hate and kill. It is not a spontaneous outburst of primordial hatred."

A Hutu Woman Remembers Exile and Tutsi Violence

Marie Béatrice Umutesi

In the following viewpoint, the author writes about her time in the refugee camp in the Democratic Republic of Congo. Many Hutus like her fled to Congo following the Tutsi takeover of Rwanda that ended the genocide. The author describes the crowded, unsanitary conditions in the camps and discusses the lack of food and the malnutrition and slow starvation of many children. She asserts that most of these people were innocent of the genocide and wonders what they have done to deserve their suffering. Marie Béatrice Umutesi is a sociologist and writer living in Belgium.

The second day after our arrival [in the refugee camp] I got to work. I knew Bukavu [in the Democratic Republic of Congo] well and had addresses of contacts, principally among the NGOs [non-governmental organizations] in my head. I very quickly found members of the Collective of Rwandan NGOs. There were about twenty of us, and later we heard that other members of the Collective had been seen on the other end of Lake Kivu at Goma. We spent a lot of time in meetings, looking for things to do, looking for ways to make ourselves useful. We contacted the local NGOs to try to assess the situation together and establish a minimal aid program for the refugees who were crammed by the hundreds of thousands—the census had not yet been made—into the streets of Bukavu, without food, without health care, without adequate sanitation.

Finding a Place to Live

First of all we had to find housing because, like everyone else, we had to take care of our families. The NGO ADI-Kivu (Action de Développement Intégré du Kivu) let us use its training center in the village of Kavumu, about thirty kilometers from Bukavu. In the beginning each family had one room, but as the number of families grew, we needed to squeeze more in, and several families had to share the same room. In the meantime, my brothers and sisters, from whom I had been separated since [the violence in the Rwandan city of] Kigali, had rejoined me. Even though there were around fifteen of us in one room, we were happy to be together again safe and sound. Few Rwandan families had the same good luck as we did. In spite of the overcrowding in which we had to live at ADI-Kivu, our situation was far better than that of other refugees, who lived in the courtyards of public building and the streets of Bukavu with no shelter from the sun and the rain. They defecated in broad daylight in holes in the ground over which someone had thrown a couple of boards to stand on. I can still see these young girls and old mothers who had to answer the call of nature in public, trying to hide their faces.

Once housed and assembled at ADI-Kivu, the Collective was able to begin work. Supervision of the thousands of unaccompanied children living in Bukavu was one of the first accomplishments. Most of the time they ate garbage and slept in the gutters or on the roofs of cars. Caritas [a Catholic humanitarian agency] and UNICEF [the United Nations Children's Fund], which were ready to put money and expertise to work for these children, tried to count and assemble them. Caritas negotiated with the local authorities to find land, and the Collective equipped it and organized the reception. It was comforting to see these children, brought from Bukavu in a state of unspeakable misery, covered in rags and filth and ulcers, their hair full of lice and traumatized by all that they had lived through in Rwanda, become the children that they had been before knowing the horrors of war, genocide, and exile. To see them play something besides war games; to hear them laugh like children should laugh, without the blank stare of those who have watched their families slaughtered; to see them run, gamboling like young goats, warmed our hearts, although at the beginning many of them hid in corners and didn't even want to open their mouths. . . .

Moving into the Camp

By the end of August, the majority of the refugees had been installed in the camps. There were between 350,000 and 500,000 Rwandans and Burundians crammed into about twenty camps in the areas of Bukavu and Uvira.

After a failed attempt to relocate a small group of refugees to Bunyakiri, in which members of the Collective were attacked by a crowd of people who suspected them of having been sent by the RPF to repatriate them to Rwanda, we realized that in order to organize in the camps, we had to live there. Since we couldn't start everywhere at the same time, we chose the two camps that were closest to ADI-Kivu: INERA and Kashusha. I therefore left the relative comfort of the room in ADI-Kivu that I shared with my family and went to live at INERA.

INERA was located about thirty kilometers from Bukavu toward Goma, and, along with the neighboring camps of Kashusha and ADI-Kivu, housed a third of the refugee population of South Kivu. Groupe Jérémie, a Zairian human rights NGO, had offered their services to Caritas for managing the camp. They let me use a small plastic blindé located in an area that the refugees had nicknamed "the neighborhood of the prefects" because it was inhabited by former officials from [assassinated president Juvénal] Habyarimana's regime. Because of the fear and suspicion that ruled the camps at that time, some inhabitants of the area did not want a neighbor whom they did not know and who, in addition, was called Umutesi, a name normally associated with Tutsi. They bribed some young men from the neighborhood who took advantage of the dark to destroy my blindé, and I had to construct a new one in another part of the camp.

Privacy Was Hard to Come By

INERA was the first place where I slept in a sheeting. On this first night I had taken every precaution to protect myself from the cold, since at night the temperature could drop to 10 degrees Celsius. It was worse than I thought it would be. I was wearing pants, a flannel nightgown, a sweater, and socks, and in addition I was covered with a blanket and a thick bedspread. In spite of all these precautions the cold kept me awake most of the night. My nose and ears were frozen. Around six in the morning I was awakened by drops of water falling in my ear. I thought at first that it was raining and that the water was coming through a hole in the sheeting, but it was only the condensation of my breath during the night. My neighbors, when I told them of my early morning misadventures, advised me to put covers on the ceiling and walls of the blindé so I could protect myself from heat during the day, cold at night, and drops of water in the morning. These coverings had another great advantage in that they protected me from the curiosity of my neighbors. When night fell and lamps were lit, passersby could see everything that went on in a blindé. The covers allowed a semblance of privacy.

My blindé was both home and office and was spacious in comparison to those of my neighbors. I was able to have a small bedroom for myself, and another for Bakunda and my three nieces, the four children who had followed me. The rest of it served as an office and a meeting room. For the refugees who had some money it was always possible to make a more spacious home, but the poor, that is to say the majority, had to make do with one sheeting. In such a small space, parents and children slept on the same mat. Children had to witness fights between their parents and other scenes not normally associated with childhood. The children were not the only ones to be present for the fights and lovemaking of their parents. The neighbors were there too. As a rule, a blindé was only separated from the neighboring ones by about a yard. Since the sheeting was thin, everything that was said in one blindé was heard by all the neighbors. It was common during the night to hear all the people in one area debating the same subject as if they were all in the same room. There was an element of security in this proximity. In case there was a problem the neighbors could intervene right away. But from time to time, it was frustrating to live so publicly.

Personal Hygiene Was Difficult

Little by little I settled in, gradually discovering the other problems of life in the camps. More than one hundred of us shared one

A makeshift refugee camp on the grounds of a school in Bukavu, Zaire, is shown in August 1994. Thousands of mostly Hutu refugees from Rwanda fled to border towns such as Bukavu following the Tutsi takeover. © Mike Goldwater/Alamy.

toilet. In the absence of a rigorous cleaning schedule, it quickly became useless. People relieved themselves all around the hole. Since there were swarms of flies everywhere, I was concerned about fly-borne disease.

There were no showers in the entire neighborhood. I had to wait until night to wash myself. Every time that someone passed by with a flashlight, I stopped washing and covered myself with a towel, but since I washed in the dark, I was never sure that I was completely clean. I had to find a solution. My blindé occupied an entire three-by-four-meter area. Every household had the same amount of land, but my neighbor had a smaller blindé and had some space left over where I was able to build a small shelter. I asked some children to collect stones to put on the ground, and since there was a source of water nearby, I dug a small ditch in front of my blindé for the water. Finally I could wash myself in peace. Everyone in the area was happy about this, because they could use it too.

In the area of cleanliness there was another feminine matter about which I could do nothing. Those in charge of humanitarian aid had not thought of feminine hygiene, and during their periods women used old rags or skirts. Soap was only distributed sporadically and it was almost impossible to find enough to wash oneself and one's soiled underwear. After several days of washing with water alone, it became hard and abrasive. If you had the misfortune of having to move around during your period, you became chapped. In addition, since men ran the camp, they had not thought of private places where women could go to wash this laundry away from the eyes of passersby. We had to wash it late at night or early in the morning in front of our blindés. The bloody water snaked in little rivulets between the blindés and here and there made bloody little puddles. To add to the discomfort of the situation, many women were obliged to wash these bloody rags in the same pots in which they prepared food for their families. I couldn't help asking myself what evil we had done to be condemned to these extremities.

Malnutrition Was Rampant

Once every two weeks we received enough corn, either as grain or flour, as well as beans or lentils, salt, and oil to survive for a week at most. Malnutrition was rampant among children under five and among pregnant and nursing mothers, particularly those who lived alone and did not have the opportunity to hire themselves out to the locals. Among the many children with bloated stomachs, huge heads, and frail limbs whom I met every day at the nutrition center at INERA, I remember Muhawe, my little four-year-old neighbor. His mother had died on the way to Zaire while giving birth to his little sister. The baby had only survived her mother by a few days, and Muhawe now lived with his widowed grandmother. When Muhawe left Rwanda, he was a chubby three-year-old. Bad food and dysentery had made him into a little old man whose huge head was all you noticed. He was too weak to get up and walk even a few steps and just sat in front of his grandmother's blindé. To go back inside he crawled on his hands and knees like a baby. His grandmother brought him regularly to the nutrition center, but the diet he was given didn't have much of an effect. He either vomited it all up or else refused to swallow. When I arrived in the neighborhood, Muhawe had reached an advanced state of malnutrition. To save him, we had to find meals with meat, the only thing he still was willing to swallow and that didn't cause him to vomit. Unfortunately, the nutrition center didn't give him any, and the grandmother was too poor to buy any, even once a week. I therefore began to feed this little boy myself and prepared meals with vegetables and potatoes and made him eat them first before getting a piece of meat, in spite of his tears and nausea. The first days were the most difficult, but later he ate everything I gave him without my having to force him.

I was happy to see him get stronger and be able to cross the distance between his grandmother's blindé and mine alone, but rebellion gnawed at me. What had Muhawe and the thousands of other Rwandan children who were dying in the camps done?

Was Muhawe guilty of genocide to deserve this fate? Why was he condemned to die? One day when I was on the verge of cracking, I took a pen and began to write down everything that was in my heart. I described the suffering of Muhawe and the other children, who, like him, were starving and whose graves lined the long road into exile. I described the tragedy of the old women who lived alone in plastic blindés riddled with holes, and the suffering of the street children of Bukavu who lived by begging. I imagined the horror experienced by the young RPF, [Rwandan Patriotic Front—the Tutsi rebel force] soldier who, back from the war, found that the militias had exterminated his entire family. I spoke of the murder of my cousin Laurent and my mother's friend Nyirarukwavu. I made a habit of writing so that people could know and break their silence, but also to stop my own pain. I often wept while I wrote, but when I had finished I felt comforted.

Organizations to Contact

The editors have compiled the following list of organizations concerned with the issues debated in this book. The descriptions are derived from materials provided by the organizations. All have publications or information available for interested readers. The list was compiled on the date of publication of the present volume; the information provided here may change. Be aware that many organizations take several weeks or longer to respond to inquiries, so allow as much time as possible.

Amnesty International
5 Penn Plaza, 14th Floor
New York, NY 10001
(212) 807-8400 • fax: (212) 463-9193
e-mail: aimember@aiusa.org
website: www.amnestyusa.org

Amnesty International is a global human rights organization that seeks to promote and protect the basic rights of all individuals worldwide. It envisions a world in which every person enjoys all of the human rights enshrined in the Universal Declaration of Human Rights and other international human rights standards. It publishes reports on its advocacy work and about areas of concern throughout the world. Amnesty International's website includes reports and news items, including specific information related to human rights issues in Rwanda.

Embassy of Rwanda
1875 Connecticut Ave. NW, Suite 418
Washington, DC 20009
(202) 232-2882 • fax: (202) 232-4544
website: www.rwandaembassy.org

The Rwandan embassy to the United States offers information and services to Rwandans and potential visitors to Rwanda. Its website also provides cultural information about Rwanda, including the genocide as well as news and events. Detailed information regarding visa processes and fees is listed here as well for those who are interested in traveling to Rwanda.

Foundation Rwanda
75 Varick Street, 5th Floor
New York, NY 10013
e-mail: info@foundationrwanda.org
website: www.foundationrwanda.org

Founded in 2008, Foundation Rwanda seeks to address the needs of the twenty thousand children born of rapes during the Rwandan genocide, as well as the needs of their mothers. The organization seeks to provide education for these children and psychological and medical support to the mothers, many of whom contracted HIV/AIDS and were shunned from their families following their rapes. The organization also seeks to help these mothers find employment.

Genocide Watch
PO Box 809
Washington, DC 20044
(202) 643-1405
e-mail: communications@genocidewatch.org
www.genocidewatch.org

Genocide Watch aims to "predict, prevent, stop, and punish genocide and other forms of mass murder" by raising awareness of the eight-stage process of genocide and by influencing international policy to curtail potential and actual acts of genocide. Its website includes news alerts and annual reports on countries at risk due to a growing likelihood of genocide or other atrocities. The website also offers links to reports issued by other members of the International Alliance to End Genocide, an international coalition of similar organizations coordinated through Genocide Watch.

Human Rights Watch
350 Fifth Ave., 34th Floor
New York, NY 10118-3299
(212) 290-4700 • fax: (212) 736-1300
e-mail: hrwnyc@hrw.org
website: www.hrw.org

Founded in 1978, this nongovernmental organization conducts systematic investigations of human rights abuses around the world and actively advocates for human dignity. It publishes many books and reports on specific countries and issues, as well as annual reports and other articles. Its website includes numerous discussions of human rights and international justice issues, including a special section on Rwanda.

Institute for the Study of Genocide (ISG)
John Jay College of Criminal Justice
899 Tenth Ave., Room 325
New York, NY 10019
e-mail: info@instituteforthestudyofgenocide.org
website: http://studyofgenocide.org

The ISG is an independent nonprofit organization established in 1982 that promotes and disseminates scholarship and policy analyses on the causes, consequences, and prevention of genocide. It publishes a semiannual newsletter and holds periodic conferences; maintains liaison with academic, human rights, and refugee organizations; provides consultation to representatives of media, governmental, and nongovernmental organizations; and advocates the passage of legislation and administrative measures related to genocide and gross violations of human rights.

Montreal Institute for Genocide and Human Rights Studies
Concordia University
1455 De Maisonneuve Blvd.
West Montreal, Quebec H3G 1M8
Canada
(514) 848-2424, ext. 5729 or 2404 • fax: (514) 848-4538
website: http://migs.concordia.ca

Founded in 1986, the Montreal Institute for Genocide and Human Rights Studies (MIGS) monitors native-language media for early warning signs of genocide in countries deemed to be at risk of mass atrocities and collects and disseminates research on the historical origins of mass killings. The institute houses the Will to Intervene Project, a research initiative focused on the prevention of genocide and other mass atrocities. The institute's website provides numerous links to information on genocide and related issues, as well as specialized sites organized by nation, region, or case.

Prevent Genocide International (PGI)
1804 S Street NW
Washington, DC 20009
(202) 483-1948 • fax: (202) 328-0627
e-mail: info@preventgenocide.org
website: www.preventgenocide.org

PGI is a global education and action network established in 1998 with the purpose of bringing about the elimination of genocide. In an effort to promote education on genocide, PGI maintains a multilingual website for the education of the international community. The website maintains a database of government documents and news releases, as well as original content provided by members.

Republic of Rwanda Website
website: www.gov.rw

The Republic of Rwanda operates a website describing the government's branches and services. It includes pages about the history and geography of the country, as well as information for potential visitors to Rwanda and Rwandan citizens. The website has pages about the Rwandan genocide and descriptions of the government structures that support justice and reconciliation, as well as peacebuilding and security.

SURF: Survivor's Fund

35 Westholm
London NW11 6LH
United Kingdom
+44 (0)20-7617-7121
e-mail: enquiries@survivors-fund.org.uk
website: http://survivors-fund.org.uk

This organization, founded by a British citizen of Rwandan origin, offers aid to survivors of the Rwandan genocide. SURF's website provides information on its ongoing activities aimed at rebuilding the lives of survivors, the organization's history, and news related to the genocide. The website also provides education materials and lesson plans based on filmed and written testimonials supported by SURF.

US Department of State

2201 C Street NW
Washington, DC 20520
(202) 647-4000
website: www.state.gov

The US Department of State is the agency of the federal government responsible for foreign affairs. The website includes daily press briefings, reports on policy issues, and numerous other articles. The office of the historian includes historical information and fact sheets on Rwanda.

World Without Genocide
William Mitchell College of Law
875 Summit Ave.
St. Paul, MN 55105
(651) 695-7621
e-mail: info@worldwithoutgenocide.org
website: http://worldwithoutgenocide.org

World Without Genocide works to protect innocent people around the world. It aims to fight racism and prejudice, advocate for the prosecution of perpetrators, and remember those whose lives and cultures have been destroyed by violence. Its website includes links to resources and discussions of numerous genocides and conflicts, including reports on Rwanda.

List of Primary Source Documents

The editors have compiled the following list of documents that either broadly address genocide and persecution or more narrowly focus on the topic of this volume. The full text of these documents is available from multiple sources in print and online.

The Arusha Accords, August 4, 1993

The peace agreement signed by the Hutu-controlled Rwandan government and the Tutsi-led Rwandan Patriotic Front ending a three-year civil war and establishing a power-sharing transitional government.

The Constitution of Rwanda, 2003

This document replaced the Rwandan constitution of 1991 and established a presidential system of government with three branches. In the preamble, the genocide is condemned and offered as a reason for implementing the new constitution and government structure.

Convention Against Torture and Other Cruel, Inhuman, or Degrading Treatment or Punishment, United Nations, 1974

A draft resolution adopted by the United Nations General Assembly in 1974 opposing any nation's use of torture, unusually harsh punishment, and unfair imprisonment.

Convention on the Prevention and Punishment of the Crime of Genocide, December 9, 1948

A resolution of the UN General Assembly that defines genocide in legal terms and advises participating countries to prevent and punish actions of genocide in war and peacetime.

Peace Agreement Between Democratic Republic of the Congo and Rwanda, 2002

Also called the Pretoria Agreement, Rwanda agreed to remove its troops from the Democratic Republic of the Congo (DRC) in exchange for the DRC agreeing to disarm remaining Hutu militia fighters from the former government who had taken shelter there.

Principles of International Law Recognized in the Charter of the Nuremberg Tribunal, UN International Law Commission, 1950

After World War II (1939–1945), the victorious allies legally tried surviving leaders of Nazi Germany in the German city of Nuremberg. The proceedings established standards for international law that were affirmed by the United Nations and by later court tests. Among other standards, national leaders can be held responsible for crimes against humanity, which might include "murder, extermination, deportation, enslavement, and other inhuman acts."

Report of the Independent Inquiry into the Actions of the United Nations During the 1994 Genocide in Rwanda, 1999

Following the failure of the United Nations to adequately prevent the Rwandan genocide in 1994, an inquiry was undertaken to determine the reasons for this failure. This report was presented to the UN Security Council in December 1999.

Rome Statute of the International Criminal Court, July 17, 1998

The treaty that established the International Criminal Court. It established the court's functions, jurisdiction, and structure.

UN General Assembly Resolution 96 on the Crime of Genocide, December 11, 1946

A resolution of the United Nations General Assembly that affirms that genocide is a crime under international law.

Universal Declaration of Human Rights, United Nations, 1948

Soon after its founding, the United Nations approved this general statement of individual rights it hoped would apply to citizens of all nations.

Whitaker Report on Genocide, 1985

This report addresses the question of the prevention and punishment of the crime of genocide. It calls for the establishment of an international criminal court and a system of universal jurisdiction to ensure that genocide is punished.

For Further Research

Books

J.J. Carney, *Rwanda Before the Genocide: Catholic Politics and Ethnic Discourse in the Late Colonial Era*. New York: Oxford University Press, 2013.

Thierry Cruvellier, *Court of Remorse: Inside the International Criminal Tribunal for Rwanda*, Chari Voss, trans. Madison, WI: University of Wisconsin Press, 2010.

Philip Gourevitch, *We Wish to Inform You That Tomorrow We Will Be Killed with Our Families*. New York: Picador, 1999.

Jean Hatzfeld, *Machete Season: The Killers in Rwanda Speak*, Linda Coverdale, trans. New York: Farrar, Strauss and Giroux, 2006.

Mahmood Mamdani, *When Victims Become Killers: Colonialism, Nativism and the Genocide in Rwanda*. Princeton, NJ: Princeton University Press, 2014.

Deborah Mayerson, *On the Path to Genocide: Armenia and Rwanda Re-Examined*. New York: Berghahn, 2014.

Filip Reyntjens, *Political Governance in Post-Genocide Rwanda*. New York: Cambridge University Press, 2013.

Jason Stearns, *Dancing in the Glory of Monsters: The Collapse of the Congo and the Great War of Africa*. New York: PublicAffairs, 2012.

Scott Straus, *The Order of Genocide: Race, Power, and War in Rwanda*. Ithaca, NY: Cornell University Press, 2013.

Susan Thomson, *Whispering Truth to Power: Everyday Resistance to Reconciliation in Postgenocide Rwanda*. Madison: University of Wisconsin Press, 2013.

Periodicals and Internet Resources

Sara J. Bloomfield and Michael Abramowitz, "Don't Assume That the Rwandan Genocide Couldn't Happen Today," *New Republic*, April 7, 2014. www.newrepublic.com.

Isobel Coleman, "Rwanda: Road to Recovery," Council on Foreign Relations, April 7, 2010. www.cfr.org.

Alan Cowell, "20 Years After, Rwanda Pauses to Recall Carnage," *New York Times*, April 7, 2014. www.nytimes.com.

Michael Crowley, "Susan Rice, Samantha Power, Rwanda and Libya," *Time*, March 24, 2011. http://time.com.

The Economist, "The Genocide in Rwanda: The Difficulty of Trying to Stop It Ever Happening Again," April 8, 2009. www.economist.com.

The Economist, "Rwanda Since the Genocide: The Road Out of Hell," March 25, 2004. www.economist.com.

Mia Fineman, "Children of Bad Memories," *Slate*, June 10, 2009. www.slate.com.

Stephen D. Goose and Frank Smyth, "Arming Genocide in Rwanda: The High Cost of Small Arms Transfers," *Foreign Affairs*, September–October 1994. www.foreignaffairs.com.

Philip Gourevitch, "After the Genocide," *New Yorker*, December 18, 1995. www.newyorker.com.

Swanee Hunt, "The Rise of Rwanda's Women," *Foreign Affairs*, May–June 2014. www.foreignaffairs.com.

IRIN, "Rwanda: Census Finds 937,000 Died in Genocide," April 2, 2004. www.irinnews.org.

Mwangi S. Kimeyi, "Is Rwanda Exportable?," Brookings Institution, October 31, 2012. www.brookings.edu.

Robert Krueger, "The Paul Kagame I Knew," *Foreign Policy*, August 5, 2010. www.foreignpolicy.com.

Mark Landler, "Declassified UN Cables Reveal Turning Point in Rwanda Crisis of 1994," *New York Times*, June 3, 2014. www .nytimes.com.

Tristan McConnell, "One Man's Rwanda," *Columbia Journalism Review*, February 1, 2011. www.cjr.org.

Charles V. Peña, "Murder Most Foul: To Stop Genocide, the US Must Learn to Intervene More Carefully," Cato Institute, November 6, 2002. www.cato.org.

Anna Polonyi, "Confronting Ghosts," *Foreign Policy*, March 17, 2014. www.foreignpolicy.com.

Laura Seay, "Rwanda: Has Reconciliation by Legal Means Worked?," *Washington Post*, April 8, 2014. www.washing tonpost.com.

Paul B. Stares and Anna Feuer, "Atrocity Prevention Since the Rwandan Genocide," Council on Foreign Relations, April 7, 2014. www.cfr.org.

Jason Straziuso, "Rwanda Orphans School Teaches Unity Post-Genocide," *Salon*, April 11, 2014. www.salon.com.

Websites and Video

Genocide Archive Rwanda (www.genocidearchiverwanda .org.rw). This website hosts a collection of video testimony related to the 1994 genocide recorded by survivors and per-petrators. The site also includes transcripts, maps, and other materials about atrocities in Rwanda.

FRONTLINE: Ghosts of Rwanda (directed by Greg Barker and Daren Kemp). A documentary first aired by PBS ten years after the genocide shows interviews with politicians, diplo-mats, and survivors.

Rwandan Stories (www.rwandanstories.org). This online col-lection of video, photography, and journalism explores the origins, details, and aftermath of the Rwandan genocide from the perspectives of survivors and perpetrators.

Index

RPF complicit in death of,
97–98
Haiti, 159
Hakizimana, Christophe, 106–107
Harroy, Jean Paul, 44
Hélène, Jean, 172
Herman, Edward S., 86–98, 100,
108
Hilsum, Lindsey, 54–57
*The History and Sociology of
Genocide* (Chalk, Jonassohn),
9–10
Hitler, Adolf, 5, 10
HIV infections, 149
Hogg, Nicole, 143
Hourigan, Michael, 97
Human rights abuses, 39, 60, 75,
102
Human Rights Watch
on need for diplomatic inter-
vention, 156–157
French support for, 127–128
genocide deniers and, 87
male gendercide and, 146
on reprisal killings, 150
Rwandan genocide report, 165
violence against women, 148
Hunter, Jane, 125–130
Hutu ethnic group
anti-Tutsi rhetoric, 29–30
French support of, 127–128
introduction, 10–11
post-independence govern-
ments, 26
slaughtering by, 25, 33–35
Tutsi violence, personal narrative, 191–198
as victims, controversy over,
106–108
Western failure to intervene
and, 156–162

Hutu Power (group), 29–30, 32,
35, 50, 87, 97, 107–108, 165, 171,
176
Hutu Ten Commandments, 133

I
INERA refugee camp, 193, 194,
197
Ingabire, Victoria, 123
Interahamwe (paramilitary force),
33, 107, 137–139, 166
Intergovernmental Association for
African Development (IGAAD),
119
International Commission of
Inquiry into Human Rights
Abuses in Rwanda, 102
International Criminal Court
(ICC), 8
International Criminal Tribunal
for Rwanda (ICTR)
Akayeshu, Jean-Paul, sentenc-
ing, 76–81
conspiracy question and, 105
conviction of perpetrators by,
140
creation of, 39
Habyarimana assassination evi-
dence, 31
Hutu military officers, trial of,
87
suppression of key verdict,
91–93
International Criminal Tribunal
for the Former Yugoslavia
(ICTY), 92, 188
International Federation of
Human Rights, 87, 165
International intervention
early warnings ignored,
165–167
overview, 164–165